The First

American Frontier

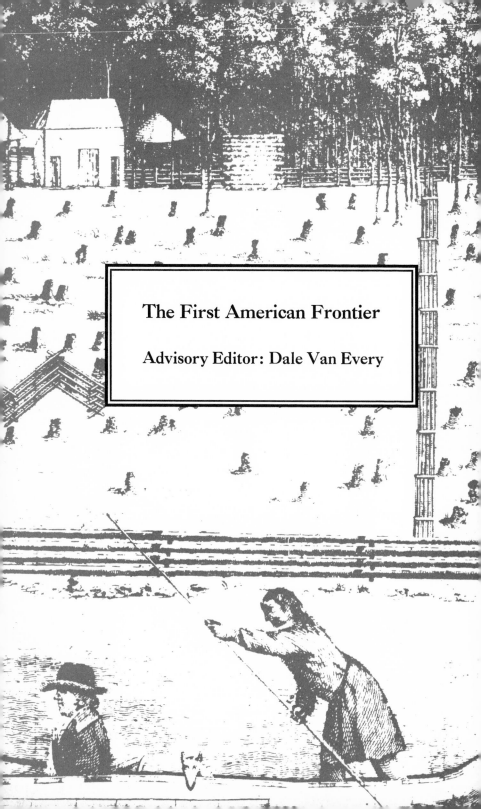

The First American Frontier

Advisory Editor: Dale Van Every

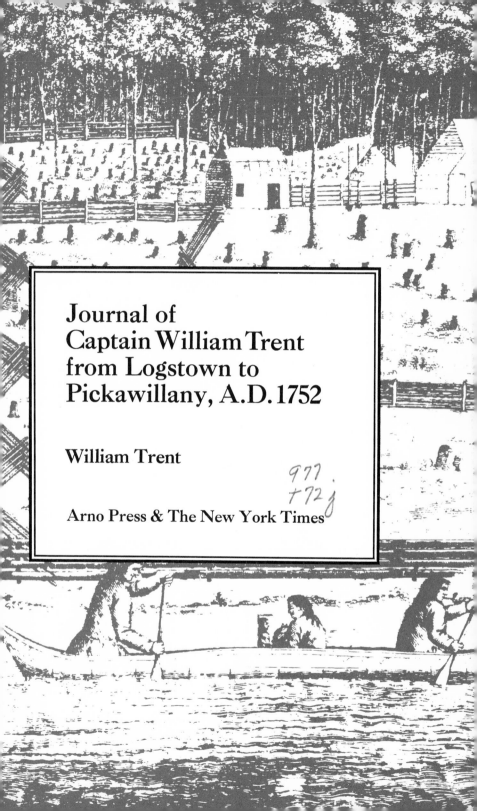

Journal of
Captain William Trent
from Logstown to
Pickawillany, A.D. 1752

William Trent

977
+72j

Arno Press & The New York Times

EG

Reprint Edition 1971 by Arno Press Inc.

Reprinted from a copy in
The State Historical Society of Wisconsin Library

LC #   79-106114
ISBN 0-405-02894-6

The First American Frontier
ISBN for complete set: 0-405-02820-2

See last pages of this volume for titles.

Manufactured in the United States of America

JOURNAL

OF

CAPTAIN WILLIAM TRENT

FROM

Logstown to Pickawillany

A. D. 1752.

NOW PUBLISHED FOR THE FIRST TIME FROM A COPY IN THE ARCHIVES OF
THE WESTERN RESERVE HISTORICAL SOCIETY, CLEVELAND, OHIO,
TOGETHER WITH LETTERS OF

GOVERNOR ROBERT DINWIDDIE

AN

HISTORICAL NOTICE OF THE MIAMI CONFEDERACY OF
INDIANS; A SKETCH OF THE ENGLISH POST
AT PICKAWILLANY

WITH

A Short Biography of Captain Trent

AND OTHER PAPERS NEVER BEFORE PRINTED

c. 1

EDITED BY

ALFRED T. GOODMAN
Secretary W. R. Historical Society

CINCINNATI
PRINTED BY ROBERT CLARKE & CO., FOR WILLIAM DODGE
1871.

INTRODUCTION.

PRIOR to the year 1660, the British colonies in America were under the management of the Lords of the King's Privy Council. On the fourth of July, the year aforesaid, Charles the Second appointed ten gentlemen from the nobility and aristocracy of his household a "Board of Trade and Plantations," and empowered any three or more of them to act as a committee in all matters pertaining to his colonies in America. The official correspondence was conducted by them, and they received and reported upon memorials, petitions, and other papers affecting the provinces. In time this board became one of great power and usefulness. It controlled the trade and commerce of the English nation, and exerted an influence in all parts of the globe, until, by royal orders, it ceased to exist in 1782. Sixty years afterward, the large mass of manuscripts which had been accumulated by the board were deposited in the British State Paper Office at London. These valuable documents, extending over a period of more than a century, have been neatly arranged according to date, and bound in volumes, each provided with a full printed index.

While investigating the early occupation of the Ohio country by the French and English, our attention was particularly directed to the many conflicting statements regarding the English post, generally known as Pickawillany. The more we examined into its history the greater our confusion; historians disagreed as to dates, and some even expressed doubts whether such a place ever existed, although EVANS and OTTEN had distinctly located it on their maps, published in 1755.

The information in HOWE's "Historical Collections of Ohio," TAYLOR's "History of Ohio," and ATWATER's "History of Ohio," regarding Pickawillany, is quite meagre; altogether, what is published in those works would make less than a page like this.

Regarding the establishment of Pickawillany and its subsequent capture by the French as events of peculiar interest to every student of
Ohio history, and believing that papers existed among the English
Archives which would throw light upon the same, we applied to the
American minister at London to extend his good offices in procuring
copies of all such papers. How cheerfully the request was complied
with is shown by the following letter from Mr. MOTLEY.

LEGATION OF THE UNITED STATES.

LONDON, *5th December*, 1870.

DEAR SIR:—With respect to your letter to me of the 24th of October last, I have
now the pleasure to transmit herewith copies of certain papers relating to the trading
post called "Pickawillany," which was attacked and destroyed by the French in the
year 1752. These documents have been kindly furnished to me by Earl GRANVILLE,
Her Majesty's Principal Secretary of State for Foreign Affairs, and are described, respect-
ively, as follows:

"Board of Trade, Virginia, No. 20, w. 89.
"   "   No. 20, w. 92.
"   "   No. 20, w. 95.
"   "   No. 39, h. 5–7.
"   "   No. 39, pp. 20–22.

Earl GRANVILLE informs me that these are all the dispatches which appear to have
passed between the Governor of Virginia and the Home Government of the day rela-
tive to the capture in question.

Trusting that these papers will prove acceptable to your society, and assuring you
that I have had much pleasure in procuring them at your request, I am, dear sir,

Your very obedient servant,

JOHN LOTHROP MOTLEY.

A. T. GOODMAN, ESQ.
Secretary Western Reserve Historical Society, Cleveland, Ohio.

The value of the papers referred to will be manifest when it is stated
that they have never appeared in print. As a contribution to our early
history they become interesting and important.

In furnishing MS. for the printer, the originals have been followed
verbatim et literatim. The notes are submitted without remark. A
short notice of Captain TRENT is given, as also a brief sketch of the
history of Pickawillany, and a somewhat extended notice of the Miami
Confederacy.   A. T. G.

The Miami Confederacy.

WHEN the French Jesuits* first traversed the Great West, they described in their Relations the numerous nations and tribes of Indians through whose country they passed. The principal among these was said to be the Miamis, whose various bands occupied that part of Ohio west of the Scioto, nearly all of Indiana, and a large portion of Illinois. About the middle of the seventeenth century, the Miami Confederacy was in the zenith of its power. It was composed of many tribes under the same form of government, each tribe with a particular chief or king, one of which was chosen indifferently from either tribe, to rule the whole nation, and was vested with greater authority than any of the others. The dominions of these kings is thus described by the celebrated chief, Little Turtle:

"My forefather kindled the first fire at Detroit; from

---

* A religious order, attached to the Roman Catholic Church, established at Rome soon after the Reformation, by Ignatius Loyola.

thence he extended his lines to the head waters of the Scioto; from thence to its mouth; from thence down the Ohio to the mouth of the Wabash; and from thence to Chicago over Lake Michigan. These are the boundaries within which the prints of my ancestors' houses are everywhere to be seen."

In 1670, the principal towns of the Miamis were on the Great and Little Miami in Ohio, on the Miami of the lakes and its tributaries, and on the Wabash. They then numbered over two thousand families, with a large array of fighting men. It was about that time that the Jesuit priests first appeared among them. The Iroquois or Five Nations had early become attached to the English. The Miami Confederacy soon became allied to French interests. We find traders among them as far back as 1680. During that year and the following one, La Salle and Hennepin* were with them, and bartered for fur skins. La Salle invited the nation to send representatives to Montreal to see the governor of Canada, assuring them of a cordial welcome by the French. In

---

* Louis Hennepin, a French Missionary, was born in 1640; embarked for Quebec in 1675, and during six or seven years explored Canada and Louisiana. In 1680 he was taken prisoner one hundred and fifty leagues from the mouth of the Illinois, and carried into the country of the Naudowessies and Issati. He gave the name of the falls of St. Anthony, and the river St. Francis. He published Description de la Louisiane, 12mo., 1683; the same in Dutch, 1688; New Discovery of a Vast Country in America, with a continuation, 1698. Nouveau Voyage dans l'Amerique, Sept., 12mo., 1711 et 1720.—*Schoolcraft.*

1681, the Iroquois were at war with the Illinois, a nation near the Mississippi, whom they subjugated in their own country. Upon returning the Iroquois were inclined to attack the Miamis, but from some cause desisted, and proceeded eastward to their hunting grounds. Acting upon the invitation of M. de La Salle, who had bestowed many presents among the nation, during the summer of 1682, the Miamis sent deputies to Montreal to meet Count de Frontenac,* the governor of Canada. The meeting took place on the 11th of August, 1682, the Indians being received with much ceremony. A treaty of amity and good will was agreed upon. The French promised assistance to the western tribes against the depredations of the Iroquois. The deputies of the Miamis had hardly returned to their territory before war with the Iroquois commenced. The latter tribes were very much incensed at the friendship displayed by the Miamis for the French, and determined upon their subjugation. They sent a large force into the Ohio country, where the two nations met in conflict near the

---

* Count de Frontenac, governor-general of Canada, born 1721, succeeded Courcelles in 1678, and in the spring of the following year built upon Lake Ontario the fort which bore his name, and which afterward was known as "La Salle's Fort." He was removed in 1682, but reinstated in 1689. Died, November 28, 1698. He was the ablest of the early French governors, and contributed largely by his energy to the advancement of Canada and its people. In 1679, he urged upon the king of France the settlement of the country northwest of the Ohio, but his recommendation was not approved of.

western end of Lake Erie. The Miamis were defeated, but the Iroquois lost so many men that they were unable to follow up their triumph. A temporary peace followed, but deadly enmity existed between the antagonists. Hostilities reopened in 1687, and continued for six years with varying fortune, but we presume as the Miamis still held their territory, they achieved a virtual triumph. In 1693, the governor of New York* sent a large present of goods to the Miamis, and invited them to a council, in the hope of separating them from the French. These presents were conveyed by the Mohegans,† but the object wholly failed. Instigated by the English, the Iroquois, in 1696, again made war upon the Miamis, when another of those long and desperate conflicts occurred, so remarkable in the wars of the Five Nations. In 1697, a bloody engagement

---

* Benjamin Fletcher.

† The Mohegans were a numerous tribe of Indians, who possessed a considerable part of the present territory of Connecticut, at the time of the first arrival of the English. According to Dr. Edwards, their language abounded with labials; had no diversity of gender, either in nouns or pronouns, and no adjectives; and seemed to be radically different from the language of the Mohawks of New York. Although these nations of Indians lived at no great distance apart, there was not to be found one word in either language which had any analogy to the corresponding word in the language of the other. The Mohegans were distinguished by their friendship to the white people. The remnant of this tribe, together with the Stockbridge Indians, migrated and settled near Lake Oneida, in the State of New York.—*McIntosh's Book of Indians.*

took place between the Senecas* and Miamis, which resulted in the complete defeat of the Senecas. For more than three years the Miamis followed up this triumph with a hatred and animosity perhaps unequaled in the annals of Indian warfare. The Senecas were obliged to repair to their fortified towns,† and their brethren of the Iroquois kept near the eastern boundaries of their territory. So terrible was the vengeance of the Miamis that the Iroquois asked a council with the English governor at Albany, and begged the aid and protection of him and his people against their depredations. The governor explained the impossibility of his furnishing troops, and advised the Iroquois to ask their enemies to a meeting, and, if possible, consummate a speedy and honorable peace. The haughty Iroquois would agree to no such course, upon which the Earl Bellomont‡ sent some trusty half-breeds to the Miamis, inviting them to trade with the English, but upon the advice of M. de Cadillac, commandant at Detroit, the English messengers were sent to Canada as prisoners. The western boundary line of the Iroquois reached to the eastern

---

*The Senecas were one of the Five Nations, afterward called the Six Nations, and lived in Western New York and Northwestern Pennsylvania.

† The Indians had no earth-work fortifications. They constructed inclosures surrounded by logs, brush, and sometimes by pickets driven into the ground. Any place of defense, which would prevent a surprise, the Indians termed a fort.

‡ Governor of New York, 1699–1701, died 15th March, 1701.

limits of the Miami Nation. The Senecas occupied
the western part of the Iroquois dominion. They suffered terribly from the incursions of their hostile neigh-
bors, and long wished for that peace which their less
afflicted brethren prevented. Finally (in 1702), a
council was held between the two belligerent powers—
peace was effected, and each nation delivered to the
other the prisoners taken in battle. This termination
of a long and eventful struggle was joyfully hailed by
the English, who felt that a new avenue of trade was
opened. In July, 1702, a message was sent from the
governor of New York,* inviting the Miamis to visit
their "English Fathers" in the east. Upon the ac-
ceptance of this the nation was divided, which led to
considerable difficulty. A portion of the nation determined to hold a council with the English, upon which
a large party with their families moved to a point near
Detroit, at the northwest of Lake Erie. The dissatis-
faction became so great that a war "among themselves"
seemed unavoidable. That portion favoring the English suddenly turned upon the French and drove M. de
Jucherau, an officer from Montreal, with thirty-four
Canadians, from a settlement they had formed at the

---

*Edward Hyde (Lord Cornbury) was a son of the Earl of Claren-
don, and succeeded Lord Bellomont as governor of New York, May 3,
1702, serving until 1708, when he was removed. He was a bigoted,
intolerant aristocrat, with few friends and many enemies. Died at
Chelsea, April 1, 1723.

mouth of the Wabash. The angry tone of the French commandant at Detroit, and their Indian allies, prevented the English from gaining any advantage from this discord among the Miamis. A few representatives of the latter went to New York and received marked attention, but they declined entering into a treaty at that time. In 1705, the Marquis de Vaudreuil sent M. de Vincennes as an ambassador to the Miamis, to effect a treaty of friendship, but his efforts proved unavailing. Finding it impossible to bring their "refractory children" to terms by means of pacific measures, a resort to arms was made. M. de Cadillac marched against the towns on the Maumee, Great Miami, and Wabash, and soon perfected a peace at his own terms. The humbled tribes asked forgiveness and protection, which was promised them. The formalities of a peace were hardly concluded when a deputation of the Miamis proceeded (1708) to Albany, where they were welcomed by the English, and received presents of great value. Lord Cornbury, in writing the Board of Trade, congratulating them upon this meeting, said he had been five years endeavoring to get the Miamis to trade, and he regarded it as an event of unusual importance that a meeting, favorable to his purposes, had been held. During the four years which followed the council at Albany, the English derived considerable benefit from trade with the Miamis. These actions gave the French great uneasiness, and they were determined they should

cease. The governor of Canada again sent M. de Vincennes as his messenger, offering peace or war; the
former on terms of friendship, amity, and good will, or
the latter with a destruction of their warriors and principal towns. The Miamis wisely determined against
war, and for several years afterward gave the French
comparatively little trouble. The disorders which had
divided the nation were almost wholly healed, and a new
era dawned upon the Confederacy. A small tribe on
the Wabash, near the Ohio, alone refused to become
allies of the French. These invited the New York
traders to come among them, and it is said that as early
as 1715, the English made their way with goods to the
Wabash. In a memoir on the Indians between Lake
Erie and the Mississippi, written in 1718, we find the
following reference to the Miamis. It is probable the
writer had been posted but as to one of the tribes, or
else the figures four hundred should be about four thousand:

"The Miamis are sixty leagues from Lake Erie, and
number four hundred, all well-formed men, and well tattooed; the women are numerous. They are hard working, and raise a species of maize unlike that of our Indians
at Detroit; it is white, of the same size as the other,
the skin much finer, and the meal much whiter. The
nation is clad in deerskin, and when a married woman
goes with another man, her husband cuts off her nose
and does not see her any more. This is the only nation

that has such a custom. They love plays and dances, wherefore they have more occupation. The women are well clothed, but the men use scarcely any covering and are tattooed all over the body." In 1719, an unsuccessful attempt was made by the French to induce the Miamis to remove from the Great and Little Miamis and Wabash to the St. Joseph, near the French fort. The following year a census of the tribes on the Maumee and St. Joseph showed two thousand souls. These were heartily in the French interests. "Fifty years ago," writes Charlevoix,* in 1721, "the Miamis were settled at the south end of Lake Michigan, in a place called Chicagon, from the name of a small river which runs into the lake, and which has its source not far from the river of the Illinois. They are divided into three villages ; one on the river St. Joseph, the second on another river which bears their name and runs into Lake Erie, and the third upon the Ouabache, which runs into the Mississippi. These last are more known by the name of the Ouyatonon ."

In July, 1723, a party of Miamis who had become

---

* Born at St. Quintin, in France, 1684. Entering the Society of the Jesuits, he became a teacher and author of great reputation. His history of New France is a peculiarly valuable work, as he visited the country which he describes, and made himself acquainted with its geography, and the manners and customs of the Indians. On one of his voyages, Charlevoix passed through the Ohio country, and has described a portion of it.

dissatisfied with the French visited New York, with an
interpreter, and asked the English to come to their
country with goods. They stated that they lived upon
" the branches of the Mississippi." The English seem to
have taken advantage of the opportunity presented, for
in 1725, we find the governor of Montreal complaining
that "the English have built two houses and some
stores on a little river which flows into the Ouabache,
where they trade with the Miamis and the Ouyatonons."
As the New York traders to reach the Miami country
passed through that of the Iroquois, the French devised
a plan, which, if successful, would soon have ridden
them of the English encroachments. They proposed
that the Miami Confederacy make war upon the Iroquois,
who had, in 1712, become powerfully reinforced by the
admission to their ranks of the Tuscaroras.* The
Miamis declined the proposal, much to the dishearten-
ment of its advisers. In 1733, a number of the Wabash
Miamis killed three French traders in an affair of trade.
For this the commandant at Detroit determined to
punish them. He accordingly sent M. de Arnaud with
a suitable force, but when the officer arrived at his des-

---

*The Tuscaroras lived in North Carolinia, about the head waters of
the Neuse and Tar. They were a savage people, made war on the
colonists, and were defeated and expelled. In 1712, they emigrated
northward and joined the Iroquois, who afterward were known as the
Six Nations. They were assigned to Eastern Ohio, and above the head
waters of the Ohio, to Buffalo, New York.

tination, the offenders begged for peace, which was granted without loss of blood. In 1744, the Miamis entered into a covenant with the French to drive all English traders from the Ohio and its northern tributaries within their territory. This was never carried into effect. In 1745, a dispute arose with the Senecas, in which several of the latter were killed, but no general warfare followed. In 1747, the Miamis entered into the conspiracy of Nicholas, the distinguished Huron chief, who resided at " Sandosket," on the bay of that name. A plot was formed for a general extermination of the French power in the West. Seventeen tribes joined in this movement. In July, the Miamis danced the calumet* at Detroit, yet soon after seized Fort Miami, took eight Frenchmen, and destroyed the buildings. The general plans† of the conspirators were defeated by

---

*A peace dance in which smoking is introduced.

† An extended reference to these will not be out of place :

In 1745, a large party of Huron Indians belonging to the tribes of the war chief Nicholas removed from the Detroit river to lands on the north side of Sandusky bay. They were a powerful body of men; active, energetic, and unscrupulous. They had in some manner been offended by the French at Detroit, which affords the reason of their change of habitation. Nicholas, their principal chief, was a wily fellow, full of savage cunning, whose enmity, when once aroused, was greatly to be feared.

Late in the same year a party of English traders from Pennsylvania visited the village of Nicholas, and were received with marked attention. Nicholas had become an implacable enemy of the French, and was

the treachery of a squaw, who informed the commandant at Detroit of them, in time to place most of the
posts and trading houses on their guard.   In February,

---

therefore ready to make a treaty of amity and good will with the
English. He accordingly permitted the erection of a large block
house at his principal town on the bay, and suffered the traders to
remain and dispose of their stock of goods.   Once located, the English established themselves at the place, and, according to French
accounts, acquired great influence with Nicholas and his tribe.   This
influence was always exercised to the injury of the French.

On the 23d of June, 1747, five Frenchmen, with peltries, arrived
at the Sandusky town from the White river, a small stream falling into
the Wabash nearly opposite the present town of Mt. Carmel, Ill.
These Frenchmen, being wholly unaware of the presence of English
among the Hurons, were unsuspicious of danger, and counted upon the
hospitality and friendship of the Indians.   Their presence, however,
inspired anything but tokens of good will.   Nicholas was greatly irri-
tated at the audacity of the French in coming into his towns without
his consent.   The English traders noticing this feeling urged the chief
to seize the Frenchmen and their peltries.   This was accomplished on
the afternoon of the day of their arrival.   The fate of the poor
Frenchmen was soon determined.   Nicholas condemned them to death,
and they were tomahawked in cold blood.   Their stock of peltries
were disposed of to the English, and by them sold to a party of Seneca
Indians.

The news of these outrages created much feeling among the French
at Detroit, and especially so among the traders in the Ohio country.
As soon as the Sandusky murders came to the information of the governor of Canada, he ordered M. de Longueuil, commandant at Detroit,
to send a messenger to Nicholas demanding the surrender of the murderers of the five Frenchmen.   The demand was not complied with.

1748, the Miamis asked for peace, and obtained it. Sieur Dubuisson was sent with a number of men, and rebuilt Fort Miami. Notwithstanding the repeated

---

Three other messengers in turn followed, but were met with the same refusal. M. de Longueuil then sent a peremptory demand, requiring the surrender of the murderers, to be disposed of according to his pleasure; that the Hurons must ally themselves at once with the French, or the latter will become their irreconcilable enemies; that the French were disposed to look upon the recent murders as acts of irresponsible parties, and not of the Huron tribe, and that all English traders must leave the Indian towns forthwith.

The answer returned to these propositions amounted to a defiance, and preparations were made for an expedition against Sandusky.

The crafty Nicholas was not less active than the French. He formed a great conspiracy for the capture of Detroit and the upper French posts, and the massacre of the white inhabitants. How long this conspiracy had been brewing, we have no information; we know that by August, 1747, the Iroquois, Hurons, Outaouagas, Abenaquis, Pous, Ouabash, Sauteurs, Outaouas, Mississagues, Foxes, Sioux, Sacs, Sarastaus, Loups, Pouteouatamis, Chaouenons, and Miamis had entered into a grand league, having for its object the extermination of French dominion and authority in the West. Every nation of Indians, excepting those in the Illinois country, entered into the plan with zeal and alacrity.

Offensive operations were to commence at once. A party of Detroit Hurons were to sleep in the fort and houses at Detroit, as they had often done before, and each was to kill the people where he lodged. The day set for this massacre was one of the holidays of Penticost. A band of Pouteouatamis were commissioned to destroy the French mission and villages on Bois Blanc Island; the Miamis, to seize the French traders in their country; the Iroquois, to destroy the French

alliances with the French, the general feeling of the Miamis was that of friendship for the English. This was perhaps induced by the fact that English traders

---

village at the junction of the Miami and St. Joseph; the Foxes, to destroy the village at Green Bay; the Sioux, Sacs, and Sarastaus, to reduce Michillimacinac, while the other tribes were to destroy the French trading-posts in their respective countries, seize the traders, and put them to death.

This great conspiracy, so skillfully planned and arranged, would have been attended with a frightful loss of life, and the utter annihilation of French power, but for its accidental yet timely discovery.

It seems that a party of Detroit Hurons had struck before the other tribes were ready, by the murder of a Frenchman in the forest a few leagues from Detroit. This act was unauthorized by the Huron chiefs, who had made their arrangements for occupying the houses at Detroit, and were only waiting for the appointed time, to strike the fatal blow. So fearful were the chiefs that their object would be detected since the murder, that a council was held in one of the houses, which had been obtained for the purpose, to determine whether any change of operations was necessary. While they were in council, one of their squaws, going into the garret of the house in search of Indian corn, overheard the details of the conspiracy. She at once hastened to a Jesuit priest, and revealed the plans of the savages. The priest lost no time in communicating with M. de Longueuil, the French commandant, who ordered out the troops, aroused the people, and gave the Indians to understand that their plans had been discovered, and would be discomfited. With great alacrity messengers were dispatched to the forts and trading-posts, which put the people on their guard, and caused them to retire to places of safety. All the settlers in the vicinity of Detroit were notified to enter the fort; the post at Miami was abandoned, and relief asked for from Quebec.

sold their goods for less, by one half, than the French; for instance, while the English gave a quart of powder for a skin, the French gave but a pint, which the Indians

---

When the Hurons at Detroit found they had been detected, they sullenly withdrew, the commandant being unwilling to open actual hostilities by detaining them. Soon after this the Indian operations began, though confined to a small scale, on account of the vigilance of M. de Longueuil in apprising his countrymen of their danger. The latter part of August, 1747, a number of Frenchmen were killed at Chibarnani; eight traders were seized in the Miami country; a man named Martineau was killed near Detroit; the Sauteurs attacked a convoy of French canoes on Lake St. Clair, captured one and plundered the goods; the Outaouas killed a number of French traders residing in their country; the Foxes murdered several traders at Green Bay; a French trader was killed on the Miami; a party of Hurons attacked the inhabitants of Bois Blanc Island, and wounded three men. Five of the Hurons were captured, taken to Detroit, and heavily ironed. One was soon after killed by the people, and another committed suicide. Other murders were committed, and trading-houses destroyed, but the conspiracy had been pretty effectually broken up by its timely discovery. Soon after hostilities had commenced numbers of those who had entered the league deserted it, and craved the pardon and favor of the French. First among these were the Outaouagas, and Pouteouatamis, the latter having agreed to destroy the Bois Blanc villages. Thus weakened, the plans and efforts of Nicholas were in a measure paralyzed.

On the 22d of September, a large number of boats, containing one hundred and fifty regular soldiers, arrived at Detroit from Montreal. Upon hearing of this, Nicholas abandoned all his plans, and was ready to make peace on the best terms he could obtain. He knew that certain destruction awaited his villages, unless pardon was obtained, for

in course of time looked upon as downright robbery.
Within a month after Dubuisson had rebuilt Fort
Miami, a message was sent by several of the tribes to the

---

the French commandant was already meditating a punishment for him
and his people, for the murder of the five traders the June previous.
During the summer two chiefs of the Detroit Hurons, Sastaredzy
and Taychatin, had visited Detroit on a professed mission of friendship. They were seized and sent to Quebec to answer for the murders
committed by the Sandusky Hurons. Sastaredzy died at Quebec on the
4th of August; Taychatin was released when peace was made. Nicholas secured the pardon of himself and the Sandusky Hurons upon the
most favorable terms, that of maintaining peace in the future. The
French abandoned their demand for the murderers of the five traders,
and made no conditions as to the Indian trade with the English.
Even during the winter that followed, 1747–8, Nicholas received at
the Sandusky villages, on two occasions, a party of Englishmen from
Philadelphia, and allowed his people to trade with them. Soon after
this, Nicholas received belts and other tokens of friendship from the
English. These things came to the ear of M. de Longueuil, and
he lost no time in asking instructions from Quebec.

On the 14th of January, 1748, Nicholas sent fourteen of his warriors
to Detroit to ask for the release of the three remaining Indians captured
at Bois Blanc Island. M. de Longueuil wishing to secure Nicholas as
an ally, granted his request, and the prisoners were released.

In February, 1748, French soldiers rebuilt and again occupied the
post on the Miami. The same month, La Jonquire, governor of Canada, ordered M. de Longueuil to give Nicholas notice that no English
traders would be allowed among his people, or in the Western country,
and if any were found, they should receive notice to quit forthwith.
Agreeable to these instructions, a French officer was sent to Sandusky,
who notified Nicholas of the wishes of the governor of Canada.

Six Nations, informing them that they were desirous of entering into a friendly alliance with the English, and wished the Six Nations to communicate their desires to

---

Finding several English at the towns, the officer commanded them to leave the country, which they promised to do.

Finding himself deserted by nearly all of his allies, his power for mischief gone, and the activity and determination of the French to suffer encroachments from the English no longer, Nicholas finally resolved to abandon his towns on Sandusky bay, and seek a home farther west. On the 7th of April, 1748, he destroyed the villages and fort, and on the following day, at the head of one hundred and nineteen warriors, and their families, left for the White river in Indiana. Soon after he moved with his people to the Illinois country, locating on the Ohio, near the Indiana line, where he died, in the fall of 1748.

The stern, unyielding conduct of M. de Longueuil toward most of the tribes who had been engaged in the conspiracy produced the desired effect. By the 1st of May, 1748, the power of the league had been utterly annihilated, and nearly every nation forced to sue for peace. This result was not produced by the sword. The withholding ot supplies, the prohibition of traders, the reduction of the savages to want, not only of provisions, but of powder and ball, did much toward humbling their desire for war. In June, a proclamation was issued by the governor of Canada, granting pardon to all the tribes engaged in the conspiracy, excepting the Mississagues and Sauteurs. Those nations had committed offenses which could not be overlooked without punishment. These exceptions were afterward withdrawn, and peace was established in the Northwest. The French, however, for several years, looked with distrust upon the rebels, as they were called. The Detroit Hurons were sulky, and not inclined to carry the yoke the French placed upon their shoulders. They had formerly enjoyed

the governors of Pennsylvania and Virginia, so that they could provide a place of meeting. The Six Nations immediately' notified the governors, and matters were expedited with all possible dispatch. On the 19th of July, 1748, the meeting took place at Lancaster, Pennsylvania, between the Hon. Benjamin Shoemaker, Thomas Hopkinson, Joseph Turner, and William Logan, Commissioners of Pennsylvania, and representatives of the Six Nations, Delawares, Shawanees, Nanticokes,* and Miamis. In the speech of the latter nation, they expressed themselves as desirous of securing the friendship and alliance of their English fathers, and requested that a road be opened from their towns to the English settlements, and that a large number of traders be sent among them. In replying to the Miamis, the commissioners said: "A council road to this prov-

---

every privilege; no obstructions being placed in their way. Now they were subjected to military rule. In the general orders of the post at Detroit, June 2, 1748, we find the following:

"Should any Huron or other rebel be so daring as to enter the fort without a pass, through sheer bravado, 't would be proper to arrest him and put him to death on the spot." Similar orders were issued at all French posts in the Northwest. These harsh, but necessary measures, had their lessons, and the Indians became as quiet and peaceable as ever. Thus ended the conspiracy of Nicholas.

For the facts above given, the writer is mainly indebted to the " New York Colonial Documents," and the " Colonial Records of Pennsylvania."

* A small tribe in Pennsylvania, related to the Delawares.

ince is a measure which nearly concerns you, as it is to be laid out thro' your towns, and no doubt you have thought well of this, and conceive you may depend on the sincerity of their professions, and that it may be for our mutual benefit, or you would not join with them in making this request. At your instance, therefore, and from the opinion we have of your prudence and integrity, we consent that such road may be opened, and it may be depended on that on our part it will always be kept clean, not the least obstruction shall be suffered to remain in it. In confirmation whereof, we give this string of wampum."

A treaty was made with the Miamis on the 23d of July, signed by the commissioners and the following chiefs: Cequenackqua, Assapausa, Natoecoqueha. By this covenant the Miamis became "good friends and allies of the English nation." It was also agreed that said Indian power, or any of its tribes, "shall not at any time hurt, injure, or defraud, or suffer to be hurt, injured, or defrauded, any of the subjects of the king of Great Britain, either in their person or estate, but shall at all times readily do justice and perform to them all acts and offices of friendship and good will." This treaty was of great advantage to the English, particularly the traders of Pennsylvania and Virginia, though New York, Maryland, and Carolina reaped much benefit from it.

In a message to the Pennsylvania assembly, August

24, 1748, Governor Palmer* thus refers to the new alliance: "This must necessarily strengthen the English interests in general among the Indians, contribute greatly to the security of our inhabitants in time of war, and tend considerably to enlarging our Indian trade, especially as we are assured by the Twightwee (Miami) deputies, that not less than twelve towns in their neighborhood are equally desirous with them to become our allies, and settle a correspondence with us; and that they only waited to know the success of their negotiations, when they would make like application. Should this be effected, besides the advantages already mentioned, the intercourse between the French at Canada and the Mississippi would be greatly interrupted, the nearest and most convenient passage being thro' those towns."

Early in the year 1749, the governors of Pennsylvania, Maryland, and Virginia rendered the Ohio Indians much service in clearing the trail which ran from the Miami country to the forks of the Ohio, and from thence to the mouth of Willis creek at the Potomac. This road, leading directly to the forks, was easy of access to the Pennsylvanians, who had a good horse path from that point to Harris' Ferry, where Harrisburg now stands. From thence to Lancaster and Philadelphia was a wagon road. It was very expensive to the Vir-

---

*He was president of the council, and became governor of Pennsylvania on the resignation of Governor Thomas, in 1747, and acted until November, 1749.

ginians to be obliged to carry their goods north to the forks, and from thence to the Great Miami and the Wabash. The result was the Pennsylvanians sold their goods cheaper. The Virginians complained bitterly on that account, and frequent difficulties arose between the traders of the two colonies. Acting Governor Lee* of Virginia wrote to the governor of Pennsylvania, and accused the Pennsylvania traders with endeavoring to create a feeling against those of his colony. This was but a pretense. The Indians bartered with the traders of both colonies, but as was natural, the parties who sold cheapest secured the great bulk of the traffic. During the year 1749, as appears from a report of Sir William Johnson,† the Miamis sent eleven canoes, eighty-eight men, and seventy-seven packs of skins to Oswego, New York. These probably came from the tribes living on the Maumee. It was this year that M. de Celeron, on behalf of the French monarch, led an expedition into the Ohio country, where he visited many of the Indian nations, among whom he found several English traders, who were ordered to quit the country.

---

*Thomas Lee was president of the council of Virginia, and succeeded to the government in 1749, on the death of Acting Governor Robinson. He was one of the principal proprietors in the Ohio Land Company.

† Sir Wm. Johnson, born in Ireland, 1714, came to America in 1734. For many years prior to his death he acted as the king's principal Indian agent in America. The ascendancy he gained over the aborigines was remarkable. He died June 11, 1774.

The principal object of Celeron's expedition was to take formal possession of the territory in the name of his king; to which end he deposited leaden plates at several points along the Ohio and its tributaries. Several of the plates have been recovered. The inscription on one of them is as follows: " In the year 1749, during the reign of Louis XV., King of France, W. E. Celeron, commander of a detachment sent by the Marquis de Lagalissoniere, commander in chief of New France, to restore tranquillity in some savage villages of these districts, have buried this plate* at the confluence of the Ohio and Tch-a-da-koin, this 29th July, near the river Ohio, alias ' Beautiful River,' (Belle riviere)† as a monument of our having retaken possession of the said river Ohio, and of those that fall into the same, and of all the lands on both sides as far as the sources of said rivers, as well as those of which the preceding kings of France have enjoyed possession, partly by force of arms, partly by treaties, especially by those of Riswick, Utrecht, and Aix-la-Chapelle."

Among the nations visited by Celeron, were the Miamis, who received him kindly, but withstood all his tempting offers for a treaty of amity and good will.

---

*Three of the plates have been recovered: one at Point Pleasant, one at Marietta, and one at Venango.

†The following names have been applied to this river: Ohio, Oyo, Oio, Onye, Ouabouskigon, Ouabach, Ouabache, Ouabachi, Belle riviere.

In May, 1750, Governor Hamilton,* of Pennsylvania, received the following message from the Miamis. The reference to the French means the expedition of M. de Celeron the year previous:

"The four Miami nations of Indians (part of whom were at Lancaster) desired Hugh Crawford to acquaint the Governor, James Hamilton, Esquire, that last July, about two hundred French and thirty-five French Indians came to their towns, in order to persuade them to return back to the French settlements, from whence they came, or if fair means would not prevail with them, they were to take them away by force; but the French finding they were resolved to adhere to the English, and perceiving their numbers to be great, were discouraged from using any hostile measures, and began to be afraid, lest they themselves should be cut off. The French brought them a present, consisting of four half barrels of powder, four bags of bullets, and four bags of paint, with a few needles, and a little thread, which they refused

---

*James Hamilton, born in Philadelphia, 1710; his father, Andrew Hamilton, was a distinguished lawyer, and at one time speaker of the Pennsylvania assembly. His son James was educated for the law. He held several offices of distinction before his appointment to succeed Lieutenant Governor Thomas, in 1748. Resigning in 1754, on account of difficulties with the assembly, he was again reinstated in 1759, continuing in office until 1763, when John Penn arrived as governor. For a few months during 1771, the administration again devolved upon him. Governor Hamilton died in New York, while that city was occupied by the British, August 14, 1783.

to accept of, whereupon the French and their Indians made the best of their way off, for fear of the worst, leaving their goods scattering about. But at the time of their conference, the French upbraided the Indians for joining the English, and more so for continuing in their interests, who had never sent them any presents, nor even any token of their regards to them. The Indians further desired Hugh Crawford to assure the governor of their steady friendship to the English, which they hoped would last whilst the sun and moon ran around the world. The Indians send by Hugh Crawford to the governor four strings of wampum, to confirm their message, and two strings more that the traders of Pennsylvania may be encouraged by him to go out and deal with them, and they earnestly request the favor of an answer from the governor by the said Hugh Crawford."

On the 17th of May, a meeting of the Miamis was held at George Croghan's* house in Pennsboro',

---

* George Croghan was a native of Ireland. When a young man he emigrated to America, locating at Pennsboro', on the west bank of the Susquehanna, nearly opposite Harrisburg. In 1745–6 he was a trader on the shores of Lake Erie, between the mouth of the Cuyahoga and the Hurons at " Sandosket." While thus engaged he learned several Indian languages, and acquired much influence with the savages. The Pennsylvania government employed him as agent in the Ohio country, but the French having captured his goods, and reduced him to bankruptcy, he was obliged to retire to the East. He served as captain in Braddock's expedition. In 1756, Sir William Johnson appointed him

Pennsylvania.   The following are extracts from the speeches:

"We the Twightwees [Miamis], who are now one with you, desire that the road which has lately been opened between us, being a new one, and therefore rough, blind, and not well cleared, may now be made plain, and that everything which may hinder the passage may be moved out of it so effectually as not to leave the least obstruction; and we desire this may be done, not only as far as where you live, but beyond you to the place where our brethren the English live, that their traders, whom we desire to see among us, and to deal with us for the future, may travel to us securely and with ease."

An answer was returned in these words.   "Brethren of the Twightwee [Miami] nation: You have, by your

---

deputy Indian agent, in charge Pennsylvania and Ohio Indians.   In 1760, he was at the council held by General Moncton at Fort Pitt, and the same year accompanied Major Rogers to Detroit.   In 1763, he was sent to England to consult with the ministry as to a boundary line with the Indians, and to recommend measures for future trade among them. In 1765, he made peace with the Western tribes, and the succeeding year made a settlement near Fort Pitt.   In 1768, he assisted at the treaty at Fort Stanwix.   At the beginning of the troubles with Great Britain, Colonel Croghan took strong ground in favor of the Colonists.   In the boundary controversy between Pennsylvania and Virginia, 1774-5, he sided with the Virginians.   During the Revolution he was charged with having abandoned the American cause and given aid to the British.   In June, 1778, his name appeared in a proclamation issued by the president of Pennsylvania, as "an enemy to the liberties of America."   He died at Passayunk, Pennsylvania, August, 1782.

deputies desired of us that we would open the new road
between us and you wider, and take out of it everything
that can possibly hinder our traveling safely and pleas-
antly to one another, and that the English traders may
come more amongst you; and further, that you hence-
forth put yourselves under our care, and desire we will
assist you with our counsel, and that you have entirely
laid aside Onontio,* and will no more be governed by
his counsels. We declare ourselves well pleased with
every part of your message, and will heartily join with
you in making the road perfectly clear and free from
all impediments." In August, Governor Hamilton returned the following answer to the message brought by
Hugh Crawford in May:

"Brethren of the Twightwees, or Miamis : I have
received four strings in behalf of four of your Nations,
by Mr. Hugh Crawford, and your message purporting
that a number of French and French Indians came to
your towns last summer, and by persuasions and presents, and when these were rejected, by menaces, endeav-
ored to shake your friendship for us, but all to no
purpose, and that you were determined to continue
faithful to us, and desired more traders may be sent
with goods into your country. I have repeated the
message, that you may know what was delivered to me

---

*The French, or the King of France; sometimes meant for the
French governor of Canada.

by Mr. Crawford, and in answer, I assure you, on behalf of this, and the other English governments, to whom I shall communicate your message, that we have a grateful sense of your attachment to us, and desire our alliance may be as strong as the strongest mountain, and endure while the sun shines and the rivers run. I have proposed it to some of the best of our traders to carry on commerce with you, and to sell you their goods at as easy a price as they can afford, and by all means to cultivate a good understanding with you, and they seem willing to do it; but as your towns are at a great distance from the Six Nations, and that several of your tribes seem still to be firmly attached to the French, the traders can not help expressing their apprehensions of the great danger there is in being intercepted, either in their passage to or return from your country, and that, unless some measures be concerted to preserve the road safe and commodious for their persons and effects, it will not be possible to extend their trade into a country so remote to any great degree. I mention this with the more earnestness, as I have lately received information that two of our traders, going from Loggstown to the Twightwees [Miamis], about three hundred miles from the first place, were either killed or taken by the French or Indians, and that a party of French Indians have killed fourteen of our people belonging to Carolina. I say our people, for the inhabitants of Carolina, Virginia, Maryland, this province, and New York, are all one people, and if any be obstructed, robbed, or killed, all of us are equally affected, and must resent it alike. Some other stories are likewise told us, which, if true, make it evident that the road is by no means safe to travel." "We give you four strings of wampum in acknowledgment of your professions, and thereby assure you that we desire to bind the chain of friendship between us as firm as it can possibly be." "Here give a string of four rows of wampum." "Inasmuch as the road is insecure, and the traders make a difficulty of traveling in it while it is so, we give you this belt to remove out of it everything that renders it dangerous." "Here a belt of wampum of eight rows." "There is a hearty inclination in the English governments towards all the Twightwee Nation, and it would be a pleasure to them to have an opportunity of showing you the many advantages which would accrue to you from your alliance with the English. If I receive the answer from the other governors time enough to send it this fall, I will transmit it to you, if not, you may expect it early in the spring."

"Philadelphia, 27th August, 1750."

The Miamis at this period were extremely obnoxious to the French. The Pennsylvanians sent a large number of presents in the fall of 1750, by George Croghan and Andrew Montour. For this act of attention, the English received permission to build a strong trading-house at the town on the Miami, at the mouth of Loramies creek. The principal traders at that point were mostly Philadelphians, men of considerable wealth and influence, and differed in character from the generality of factors. It was about this time that the proprietors of Pennsylvania, residing in England, offered to give four hundred pounds toward the erection of a strong fort among the Ohio Indians, and guaranteed one hundred pounds a year toward supporting it; but the Pennsylvania assembly rejected the offer upon its presentation. During the winter of 1750–51, according to Geo. Croghan, thirty Miami Indians were killed by the French. In 1751, four Pennsylvania traders, named Luke Arowin, Joseph Fortiner, Thomas Borke, and John Pathen were taken prisoners near the Maumee. Early in 1752, the Miamis suffered severely from the small-pox. During the year occurred the destruction of the English post at Pickawillany, all of which is detailed elsewhere. Soon after this, in a communication to his government, the governor of Canada expressed the opinion that, unless the alliance between the English and Miamis was broken off, the fall of Detroit would eventually ensue. In 1753, a large body of French from Canada moved to the southwest, and erected Forts Presque Isle,* Le Bœuf,† and Venango.‡ In April of that year, M. Jon-

---

*On the site of Erie, Pennsylvania.

† On the South or West fork of French creek, on the site of Waterford, Erie county, Pennsylvania.

‡ About eighty miles below the mouth of French creek, on the west side of the Alleghany river.

caire* was sent, with a small detachment of regulars and a number of friendly Senecas, to visit the Indians on the Ohio and its branches. He had full powers to treat, and was directed, if thought necessary, to demand hostages for the good conduct of all nations in alliance with the English. When Joncaire reached the Miamis, he marched into their towns with great ceremony. The Indians were frightened, and promised to "again become the children of the French."

Joncaire assured them of protection, and succeeded in inducing a large number to go with him to the fort on the Maumee. A considerable portion of the Miamis, however, adhered to the English, and in September attended a council at Winchester, Va. The following month a like conference was held at Carlisle, Pa. During the spring of 1753, the Pennsylvania and Virginia assemblies had voted large presents to the Miamis, as tokens of condolence and sympathy for their recent loss at Pickawillany. After the French appeared at Presque Isle, the governors of both provinces hesitated

---

* Joncaire had gained great influence over the Indians, having been an Indian agent for more than twenty years, and had been, says Bancroft, successfully negotiating with the Senecas. He was become by adoption one of their own citizens and sons, and to the culture of a Frenchman added the fluent eloquence of an Iroquois warrior. When the Delawares and Shawanese migrated to Alleghany, Joncaire soon found his way among them, and succeeded in persuading them to join the French.

to confer the gifts until the real intentions of the Indians were ascertained. The bulk of the intended bounty consisted of powder, lead, and flints, and was in charge of George Croghan, as agent of Pennsylvania, and Messrs. Gist, Trent, and Montour, of Virginia. When the Miamis visited Winchester and Carlisle, they expected to receive these goods, having received assurances to that effect. It is no wonder, then, that they were dissatisfied at being dismissed on their good behavior, especially after the sacrifices they had made the year previous in defending the English from the French. The Miamis felt this distrust, and soon after their return home, the great body of the nation resolved to cast their fortunes with the French. In May, 1756, war broke out between the Illinois* and Miamis, but did not long continue. Peace was arranged by ambassadors sent by the commandant at Detroit. The same year Sir William Johnson sent Kindarunte, a Seneca chief, with a belt of wampum, and a message inviting the Miamis to a council at Oswego. The invitation was

---

* The Illinois dwelt in the neighborhood of the river to which they have given their name, while portions of them extended beyond the Mississippi. Though never subjugated, they were reduced to the last extremity by the repeated attacks of the Five Nations. The Illinois suffered so much by these and other wars, that the population of ten or twelve thousand, ascribed to them by the early French writers, had dwindled, during the first quarter of the eighteenth century, to a few small villages.—*Parkman's Con. of Pontiac, Vol. I.,* 33.

declined. At this time most of the Western Indians were strong allies of the French, and assisted their armies upon various occasions. In 1757, a large body of the Miamis were as far east as Fort William Henry, and assisted the French at the capture of Fort George. The Miamis continued their alliance with the French until 1759, when the majority of the nation sought English favor. This change was produced from a feeling of discontent at repeated failures and defeats, and the loss of the posts about the head-waters of the Ohio. These the French had promised to retain. The Ohio Indians were generally at peace with the English until the year 1763, when Pontiac's* war broke out. In that short yet eventful struggle, the Miamis were with their red brethren, and assisted particularly in the destruction of Forts Miami and Sandusky. They brought into the field one thousand warriors, who strenuously opposed the occupation of the Illinois country by the English. They even carried this opposition so far as to refuse to allow a detachment from Colonel Bradstreet to march through their territory. After the failure of Pontiac, that great chief sought refuge among the Miamis, and continued with them for more than a year. In March, 1765, we find Sir William Johnson com-

---

* A distinguished chief of the Ottawa nation. He did not long survive the peace of 1763. Having immigrated to the Illinois country, he was barbarously murdered by one of his own tribe.

plaining that the Miamis took a soldier of Fort Miami prisoner, robbed him of all his clothing, and turned him into the woods. He also reports that the Miamis are at war with the Chippewas, allies of the English, and had killed and captured a large number of them. In May, George Croghan, who had been appointed Johnson's deputy, set out from Fort Pitt to make peace with all the Western Indians. On the 24th of August, attended by Colonel Campbell, he made a treaty with the Miamis, by which that nation was to remain undisturbed in its hunting grounds. Not long after this the tribes abandoned their towns on the Great Miami, and removed to the Maumee, the St. Joseph and Wabash rivers. During the revolution they adhered to the British, and gave the frontier posts much trouble. After the peace of 1783, they remained bitterly hostile to the Americans. They were the leaders in nearly all the incursions that ravaged the border settlements from 1783 till the treaty of Greenville in 1795. The disastrous campaigns of Harmar and St. Clair were especially directed against their towns. The victory of Wayne broke their power for evil, and from that time the nation seems to have gradually dwindled into insignificance. As the West began to be settled, the Miamis moved off in small bodies for the lands beyond the Mississippi, so that the once powerful confederacy became scattered and amalgamated with other tribes. Their identity is now entirely lost.

HISTORICAL SKETCH

OF THE

English Post at Pickawillany.

FOR MANY YEARS prior to the advent of English traders in the West, the Miamis had a village on the west side of the Great Miami river, at the mouth of what afterward became known as Loramies creek. That point was visited by the *Coureurs des Bois** at an early day, and had become a place of note long previous to the alliance of the Miamis with the English. From the latter it received the name of "*Tawixtwi town*," until the building of a stockade, when it was called *Pickawillany*, though in some accounts we find the name "*Picktown*" applied to it.

English traders dealt with the Miamis at an early day, even while the latter were fully pledged to French interests. The Pennsylvania factors seem to have been special favorites, for they sold their goods at half the price asked by the *Coureurs des Bois*. This was a matter

---

*Canadian voyagers, who traveled under the direction of the traders.

of importance to the Indians, and doubtless had much to do with their subsequent friendly alliance with the English. It was not, however, until the year 1747 that the Miamis withdrew from French interests. That year, the conspiracy of Nicholas occurred, which threatened for a time the annihilation of French power in the West. The Miamis were fully in the plot, and performed the part assigned them by the capture and destruction of Fort Miami, at the confluence of the St. Joseph and St. Mary's rivers. In 1748, at a treaty held at Lancaster, Pennsylvania, the Miamis fully committed themselves to the care and protection of the English, an event which was hailed with great satisfaction by the colonists, and was equally as distasteful to the French government.

In the notice of the Miami tribe, elsewhere given, full particulars of this alliance will be found. The Tawixtwi town immediately became a place of importance to the factors. A number of houses were erected for the accommodation of goods and peltries. These were ordinary log cabins, the trading being carried on below, while an "upper story" or "loft" was used as a place to stow away skins and combustible material. During the summer of 1749, M. de Celeron visited the Tawixtwi town, but found no traders there, they having had timely notice of his coming, and departed with their goods and chattels. The Miami warriors were in force at the time of Celeron's visit, and that officer did no injury. On the contrary, he treated them with kindness and attention. Presents were given, and the usual speeches made, but the Indians withstood his arts and artifices, and remained friendly to the English. While the English traders felt safe in the hands of the Miamis, they were in constant fear of the French. Occasionally an unfortunate trader became a victim. The dread of such a fate was increased by the fact that the Ottawas were known to "kill, roast, and eat" their English captives. The Miamis shared this feeling, as several of their best warriors had recently fallen into the enemy's hands. The need of a strong post was felt, which would afford better protection than the ordinary houses of the traders. It was some time, however, before the Indians would allow the erection of such a structure.

In Pennsylvania, licenses to trade with the Indians were granted by the governor upon the recommendation of the justices of the counties in which the applicant resided. No record seems to have been kept of these licenses, but from reports of George Croghan, Conrad Weiser,* and others, we have compiled the follow-

---

* A native of Herenburg, Germany, born November 2, 1696. His father, John Conrad Weiser, emigrated to America in 1710. Conrad learned the Mohawk language when a young man. In 1729, having married, he settled near the present site of Womelsdorf, Berks county, Pennsylvania. In 1731, he entered the service of Pennsylvania as an Indian interpreter. He was justice of the peace and Indian agent

ing list of persons engaged in traffic with the Miamis in Ohio, between 1745 and 1753. A portion of them probably belonged to Virginia: John Potts, John Pathen, Samuel Cozzens, Peter Chartier (licensed in Pennsylvania, afterward deserted to the French), Conrad Weiser, James Dunning, John Powle, Thomas McGee, George Croghan, James Denny, Robert Callender, George Gibson, Michael Crouse, Jacob Sclaugh, Robert Dunning, Henry Noland (or Norland), Hugh Crawford, James Lowry, Michael Cresap, Sr., Barney Currant, ———— Parker, Morris Turner, Ralph Kilgore, John Frazier, Christopher Gist, Thomas T. K. Kinton, Jacob Pyatt, John Owens, Thomas Ward, William Trent, Joseph Nelson, James Brown, Dennis Sullivan, Paul Pearce, Caleb Lamb, John Grey, John Findlay, David Hendricks, Aaron Price, Thomas Burney, Michael Taafe, Alexander McGinty, Jabez Evans, Jacob Evans, William Powell, Thomas Hyde, ———— Young, John Trotter, William Campbell, Thomas Mitchell, Sr., Reed Mitchell, William Ives, Thomas Mitchell, Jr., John Patten, William West, Luke Arowin, Joseph Fortiner, Andrew McBryer, Thomas Borke.

The traders' goods were carried on pack-horses, along the old Indian trails which led to all the principal towns and villages. The articles of traffic

for many years. During the French and English war, Governor R. H. Morris commissioned him colonel of a regiment of Berks county volunteers. He died July 13, 1760.

on the part of the whites were fire-arms, gunpowder, lead, ball, knives, flints, hatchets, rings, rum, medals, blades, leather, cooking utensils, shirts, and other articles of wearing apparel; tobacco, pipes, paint, etc. In return for these the Indians gave skins of various animals, which were made into valuable furs by Eastern merchants. It was very seldom that an Indian got the advantage of a white man in these barterings. Some of the traders would run regular "caravans" of fifteen or twenty horses, making several trips during the year. It is impossible to give any definite account of the extent of this traffic, but it must have amounted to great value. Thousands of skins were doubtless furnished by the Indians at Pickawillany and their other Ohio towns.

Having obtained permission from the Indians, the English, in the fall of 1750, began the erection of a stockade, as a place of protection, in case of sudden attack, both for their persons and property. When the main building was completed, it was surrounded with a high wall of split logs, having three gateways. Within the inclosure the traders dug a well, which furnished an abundant supply of fresh water during the fall, winter, and spring, but failed in summer.

At this time Pickawillany contained four hundred Indian families, and was the residence of the principal chief of the Miami Confederacy. Christopher Gist was there in February, 1751, and in his published journal says the place was daily increasing, and "accounted one of the strongest Indian towns on this continent." In his entry for February 18, he thus refers to the stockade: " We walked about and viewed the fort, which wanted some repairs, and the traders' men helped them to bring logs to line the middle."

In several contemporary papers we find it stated that the fort at Pickawillany was built of stone.* If this was the case, remains of the structure ought yet to be visible, but we are informed on good authority that no traces of the kind are to be found in the neighborhood of the mouth of Loramies creek. During the winter and spring of 1751, according to a letter of George Croghan, thirty of the Miamis were killed by the French. No particulars are given. In January, 1751, three French soldiers, who had deserted from the fort at the St. Joseph's and St. Mary's, delivered themselves

---

* " Oswego, 19*th July*, 1751.

" Dear Sir : As I did not know of this Bottoes going off, till just now, have but just time to acquaint you that there passed by here, a few days ago, some canoes of French traders, who say there was an army gone up the other side of the lake, with which was two hundred Orondack Indians, under the command of Mons. Belletre and Chevalier Longville, and that their design was against a village of the Twigtwees, where the English are building a trading house of stone, and that they are to give the English warning to move off in a peaceable manner, which, if they refused, they were to act with force. * * *

" Benjamin Stoddert.

" Colonel Wm. Johnson."

to the English at Pickawillany. The Miamis demanded the Frenchmen for purposes of revenge. The English refused to give them up, but were obliged to send them to George Croghan's, at Muskingum, in order to preserve their lives.*

When the governor of Canada was informed of the situation of affairs among the Miamis, he became highly exasperated, and threatened the destruction of all their towns. He was constrained from this by the advice of the commandant at Detroit, but when it became known to him that Pickawillany was a receiving point for French deserters, his anger again broke forth, and orders were given for a military force to march against the town. The murder of fifteen French traders, by the Miamis, in the spring of 1752, did not tend to allay the bitter feelings which rankled in the breast of the governor. The commandant at Detroit received

---

* Christopher Gist, in his journal, dated Muskingum, Wednesday, January 9, 1751, says: "This day came into town two traders from among the Picqualinness (a tribe of the Tawightwis), and brought news that another English trader was also taken prisoner by the French; and that three French soldiers had deserted and come over to the English, and surrendered themselves to some of the traders at the Picktown; and that the Indians would have put them to death, to revenge their taking our traders, but as the French had surrendered themselves to the English, they would not let the Indians hurt them, but had ordered them to be sent under the care of three of our traders, and delivered at this town to George Croghan."

the orders of his superior, and promptly obeyed them. In May, Monsieur St. Orr* was sent with a small party of French soldiers, a few Canadians, and a large body of Ottawa and Chippewa† allies, against the English post. M. St. Orr was directed to demand from the Indians the English traders and French deserters in their towns, and upon their failing to comply with this, the traders and deserters should be taken by force. M. St. Orr arrived before Pickawillany in June. The events which followed are narrated in the journal of Captain Trent. Suffice it to say here, the English traders, with two exceptions, were killed or captured, and a number of the Miamis fell in defending them from the enemy. The news of the disaster was conveyed to Pennsylvania by Thomas Burney, who arrived at Carlisle on the 29th of August, 1752. He reported to Captain Robert Callender,‡ a prominent Indian trader, and one of the justices for Cumberland county. On the 30th, a messenger was sent to the governor, with the following communication:

---

* Afterward distinguished in French and English war.

† The Chippewas and Ottawas were allies, and generally in the interest of the French. They lived in the neighborhood of Lakes Huron, Superior, and Michigan. The Chippewas, in 1752, numbered about five thousand warriors ; the Ottawas, about nine hundred.

‡ Afterward an officer in Bouquet's expedition against the Ohio Indians, having charge of a convoy of provisions.

"Carlisle, *August* 30, 1752.

" *May it please your Honor:*

" Last night, Thomas Burney, who lately resided at the Twightwees' town in Allegheny, came here and gives the following account of the unhappy affair that was lately transacted there: On the twenty-first day of June last, early in the morning, two Frenchmen and about two hundred and forty Indians came to the Twightwees' town, and in a hostile manner attacked the people there residing. In the skirmish there was one white man and fourteen Indians killed, and five white men taken prisoners.

" The party who came to the Twightwees' town reported that they had received, as a commission, two belts of wampum from the governor of Canada, to kill all such Indians as are in amity with the English, and to take the persons and effects of all such English traders as they could meet with, but not to kill any of them if they could avoid it, which instructions were in some measure obeyed.

" Mr. Burney is now here, and is willing to be qualified not only to this, but to sundry other matters which he can discover concerning this affair. If your Honor thinks it proper for him to come to Philadelphia to give you the satisfaction of examining more particularly in relation to it, he will readily attend your Honor upon that occasion, or make any affidavit of the particulars here.   Such orders as your Honor pleases to send on this occasion, shall certainly be obeyed by,

"May it please your Honor,

"Your Honor's most ob't serv't,

"ROBT. CALLENDER.

"P. S. Inclosed, your Honor has the Twightwees' speech to Mr. Burney, with a scalp and five strings of wampum and beaver.

"Fifteen days after the taking of the town, Thomas Burney and Captain Trent, with twenty Indians, went back to the town, where they found all the Indians were fled, and on their return met with three of their chiefs, to whom Captain Trent delivered the Virginia present, such as he had then with him.   These chiefs informed them the Indians were gone eighty miles from thence, and there would reside till they heard further from their brothers."

The message inclosed in the above was as follows:

"BROTHER ONAS: We, your brothers, the Twightwees, have sent you, by our brother, Thomas Burney, a scalp and five strings of wampum, in token of our late unhappy affair at the Twightwees' town; and whereas our brother always been kind to us, hope he will now put us in a method how to act against the French, being more discouraged for the loss of our brother, the Englishman who was killed, and the five who were taken prisoners, than for the loss of ourselves; and, notwith-

standing the two belts of wampum which were sent from
the governor of Canada as a commission to destroy us,
we still shall hold our integrity with our brothers, and
are willing to die for them, and will never give up this
treatment, although we saw our great Piankashaw King
(which commonly was called Old Britain by us) taken,
killed, and eaten within a hundred yards of the fort
before our faces. We now look upon ourselves as lost
people, fearing that our brothers will leave us; but before we will be subject to the French, or call them our
fathers, we will perish here."

Soon after the governor received these communica-
tions, he sent for Mr. Burney, but a meeting was delayed
until the winter following. In the meantime, October,
the governor sent a message to the legislature, informing them of the troubles to the westward. On account
of the lateness of the season, and the governor's desire
to first examine Mr. Burney, no action was taken by
the assembly regarding the affair at Pickawillany until
the following year. In May, 1753, the following resolution was adopted: "That the sum of two hundred
pounds be now allowed as a present of condolence to
the Twightwee nation, on the melancholy occasion mentioned in the governor's message of the sixteenth of
October last." At the same time, the assembly appro-
priated six hundred pounds, to be distributed among
the Shawanees, Wyandots, Senecas, and other Western
tribes. The government of Virginia likewise made

large appropriations for the Indians, with a special present for the Miamis at Pickawillany. The Pennsylvania goods were placed in charge of George Croghan, those of Virginia with three commissioners, Messrs. Gist, Trent, and Montour. About this time the French made their appearance at Presque Isle, LeBoeuf, and Venango, which determined the governors of both colonies to postpone the delivery of the intended presents until the intentions of the Indians regarding the movements of the French were discovered. In September, the governor of Virginia met the Miamis and other Ohio nations in council at Winchester, and in October, commissioners of Pennsylvania met them at Carlisle. The following extracts are made from the speeches of the Miamis, delivered to the council:

"You have, like a true and affectionate brother, comforted us in our affliction. You have wiped away the blood from our seats and set them again in order. You have wrapped up the bones of our warriors and covered the graves of our wise men, and wiped the tears from our eyes and the eyes of our women and children, so that we now see the sun and all things are become pleasant to our sight. We shall not fail to acquaint our several nations with your kindness. We shall take care that it be always remembered by us, and believe it will be attended with suitable returns of love and affection."

"Brother Onas: The Ottawas, Chippewas, and the French have struck us. The stroke was heavy and hard to be borne, for thereby we lost our king and several of our warriors; but the loss our brethren, the English, suffered, we grieve for most. The love we have had for the English from our first knowledge of them still continues in our breasts, and we shall ever retain the same ardent affection for them. We cover the graves of the English with this beaver blanket. We mourn for them more than for our own people." [Here was spread on the floor some beaver skins sewed together in the form of a large blanket.]

At the same meeting the Miamis thus addressed the Six Nations and their allies:

" BROTHER ONAS: This belt of wampum was formerly given to the king of the Piankashas, one of our tribes, by the Six Nations, that if, at any time, any of our people should be killed, or any attack made on them by their enemies, this belt should be sent with the news, and the Six Nations would believe it. The Twightwees [Miamis], when they brought this belt to the lower Shawanees town, addressed themselves to the Shawanees, Six Nations, Delawares, and then to the English, and said:

"*Brethren:* We are an unhappy people. We have had some of our brethren, the English, killed and taken prisoners in our towns. Perhaps our brethren, the English, may think or be told that we were the cause of their death. We, therefore, apply to you, the Shawanees, etc., to answer the English we were not.

The attack was so sudden that it was not in our power to save them. And we hope, when you deliver this speech to the English, they will not be prejudiced against us, but look on us as their brethren. Our hearts are good toward them."

The Pennsylvania commissioners replied at length. Addressing the Miamis they said: "The concern expressed by the Twightwees for death and imprisonment of the English, with their professions of love and esteem, denotes a sincere and friendly disposition, which entitles them to ourthanks and the continuance of our friendship ; this they may certainly depend on."　　*　　*

"*Brethren:* We desire you will send these two strowds* to the young king as an acknowledgment of our affectionate remembrance of his father's love to us, and of our good will to him."

" Be pleased to present to the widow of the Piankasha king, our late hearty friend, these handkerchiefs to wipe away the tears from her eyes ; and likewise give her son these two strowds to clothe him." [Here two handkerchiefs and two strowds were given.]

"*Brethren Twightwees:* We assure you we entertain no hard thoughts of you, nor in anywise impute to you the misfortune that befell the English in your town ; it was the chance of war. We were struck together, we

---

* A breech-cloth.

fell together, and we lament your loss equally with our own."

The council was closed by an address of the commissioners to all the nations assembled, respecting the goods which had been ordered as presents to the Miamis and other nations in alliance with the English. These were the goods which, at that time, were in the care of Geo. Croghan, as agent of Pennsylvania. The commissioners said:

"We have reason to think from the advices of Taafe & Callender, that it would be too great risk, considering the present disorder things are in at Ohio, to increase the quantity of goods already given you. We, therefore, acquaint you that though the governor has furnished us with a larger present of goods to put into your public store house, as a general stock for your support and service, and we did intend to have sent them along with you, we have on this late disagreeable piece of news altered our minds, and determined that the goods shall not be delivered till the governor be made acquainted with your present circumstances, and shall give his own orders for the disposal of them, and that they may lie ready for your use, to be applied for whenever the delivery may be safe, seasonable, and likely to do you the most service."

After the Indians returned to their homes, the reason of the retention of the goods was manifest. The Pennsylvania present consisted mainly of powder and lead, which was feared would be brought into requisition against them. This would certainly have been the result, for most of the Ohio Indians were soon after forced into terms by the French, and became their allies. The Six Nations remaining faithful, in due time received their share of the goods, but it does not appear that the Miamis partook of the bounty provided for them. In December, Mr. John Patten was sent by the governor of Pennsylvania to learn the intentions of the Miamis, and it appears that he reported them as "gone over to the French." At this time most of the English traders abandoned the Ohio trade. Pickawillany was wholly deserted by them. Not long after, the French commandant at Vincennes, deeming the location a good one, sent some traders to the place, and made a treaty of concord and friendship with the Miamis, lavishing upon them a very large amount of money and a great variety of costly presents. The place, however, did not possess enterprise or spirit, and was not widely known as a trading post until 1769, when a Canadian French trader, named Peter Loramie, established a store there. He was a man of energy, and a good hater of the Americans. For many years he exercised great influence among the Indians. After his arrival the town was called" Loramie's Station." During the Revolution, Loramie was in full fellowship with the British. Many a savage incursion to the border was fitted out from his supply of war material. So noted had his place become

as the headquarters of spies, emissaries, and savage bor-
derers, that Gen. George Rogers Clarke,* of Kentucky,
resolved to pay it a visit. This he did, with a large
party of Kentuckians, in the fall of 1782. The post
was taken by surprise, Loramie narrowly escaping being
made prisoner. His store was rifled of its contents
and burned to the ground, as were all the other habita-
tions in the vicinity. Poor Loramie shortly afterward
removed with a party of Shawanees to a spot near the
junction of the Kansas and Missouri. There he closed
his days. The site of Pickawillany and Loramie's Station has never been rebuilt.

---

* A distinguished soldier, born in Albemarle county, Virginia, 19th
November, 1752. Served as a captain in Dunmore's war, and a colonel
in the Revolution. Died February, 1818, near Louisville, Kentucky.
For a detailed sketch of Clarke's life and services, see Collins' History
of Kentucky.

BIOGRAPHICAL SKETCH

OF

William Trent.

WILLIAM TRENT was a native of Lancaster county, Pennsylvania, born about the year 1715. His father was distinguished in the civil history of that State, holding many positions of trust and profit. William Trent entered the service of Pennsylvania at an early day. In June, 1746, Governor Thomas* appointed him captain of one of four companies, raised in Pennsylvania, for an intended expedition against Canada. During that year he was stationed, under orders of Governor Clinton,† of New York, at Saratoga,

---

* George Thomas, a West India planter—governor of Pennsylvania, 1738–1747—a man of energy and talent. He died January 11, 1775.

† Governor of New York from 1743 to 1753. He was the youngest son of Francis Clinton, Earl of Lincoln. His administration was turbulent. He was engaged in a violent controversy with Justice Delancy and the Assembly, and with Colonel Daniel Horsemander, afterward Chief Justice. Soon after his service as executive of New York, he was made governor of Greenwich Hospital, London.

where his command did garrison and scouting duty for over a year.   During the month of April (7th), 1747, a party of two hundred French and Indians, under M. de St. Luc, appeared before Saratoga, when an encounter took place with a small force of the colonial troops. Captain Trent, with sixty men, unsuspicious of danger, had advanced some distance from the town, when his force fell into an ambuscade of the enemy.   At the first fire, eight of them fell.   Trent rallied the survivors, and bravely fought for an hour, when relief came, and M. de St. Luc was forced to withdraw.   Trent returned to Saratoga.

In December, 1747, the time of his company having expired, Captain Trent returned to Pennsylvania, where he was honorably discharged, receiving the thanks of the Assembly for his patriotic services.   On the 10th of March, 1749, he was appointed by Governor Hamilton, a justice of the court of common pleas and general sessions of the peace for Cumberland county, and discharged the duties of this position for several years. During the same year, under authority of the Assembly, he was employed as messenger to the Ohio Indians, to carry messages and presents to the principal nations. For this service he received the sum of two hundred and forty-fiv epounds.   In 1750, Captain Trent formed a partnership with the celebrated George Croghan, his brother-in-law, to engage in the Indian trade.   This firm continued in existence for over six years, and its members acquired great influence with the savages. In the extent of its mercantile operations it was unequaled in the West. In 1752, Captain Trent was employed by the governor of Virginia, as an agent of that colony, to attend the commissioners at Logstown, in their council with the Ohio tribes. While the conference was being held, he was dispatched with messages and presents to the Miamis, a full account of which will be found in his journal. In August, 1753, he was directed by Governor Dinwiddie, to examine the site selected by the commissioners, in 1752, for a fort on the Ohio. This was at the forks of the Ohio, where Pittsburg now stands. In a letter from John Frazier to an Indian trader named Young, dated "Forks, August 27, 1753," we find the following reference to Trent:

"There is hardly any Indians now here at all, for yesterday there set off along with Captain Trent and French Andrew, the heads of the Five Nations, the Picts,* the Shawanees, Owendots, and the Delawares, for Virginia; and the Half King set off to the French fort, with a strong party along with him, to warn the French off their land entirely, which, if they did not comply to, then directly the Six Nations, the Picts, Shawanees, Owendots, and Delawares were to strike them without loss of time. The Half King was to be

---

*A tribe of the Miamis was sometimes called by this name, especially by the English traders.

back in twenty days from the time he went away; so were the Indians from Virginia. Captain Trent was here the night before last, and viewed the ground the fort is to be built upon, which they will begin in less than a month's time. The money has been laid out for the building of it already, and the great guns are lying at Williamsburg ready to bring up. The French are daily deserting from the new fort. One of them came here the other day whom I sent to Captain Trent; he has him along with him to Virginia."

In September, Captain Trent was present at the treaty making at Winchester, Virginia. Under its provisions, a large quantity of ammunition and other goods were ordered for the Miami and Delaware tribes. Three commissioners were appointed to convey these presents to the Ohio: William Trent, Andrew Montour, and Christopher Gist. It does not appear that the Miamis received their portion of the goods, but the Delawares did theirs. Early in January, 1754, Governor Dinwiddie commissioned Trent to raise one hundred men for immediate service on the frontier. By the last of the month this force was raised, and immediately marched to the mouth of Redstone creek, where a temporary store house was erected for the Ohio company, in which to place articles and supplies, to be carried from thence to the mouth of the Monongahela. While at Redstone, the Captain received instructions from Governor Dinwiddie to build a fort at the forks of the

Monongahela and Ohio, with the least practicable delay, suitable in strength to resist any ordinary attack. He was further ordered to "capture or destroy any hostile or resisting force." Trent hastened at once to carry out the governor's instructions. On the 17th of February, he reached the forks and began the erection of a military post. Late in the month, intelligence came by friendly Indians that the French meditated an attack. Trent immediately wrote to the governor, apprising him of the strength of the French above, and asking that reinforcements be sent him. These were ordered by Dinwiddie, but, as subsequent events will show, too late for service. In March, George Croghan was at the forks, and in a letter to the governor of Pennsylvania, he speaks of seeing Trent and his command hard at work, building a fort, "which," he says, "seemed to give the Indians great pleasure, and put them in high spirits." About this time, a squad of Trent's men captured six French Indians, who were sent prisoners to Virginia. Early in April, Captain Trent left the fort, then uncompleted, on a visit to the mouth of Wills creek, Maryland, leaving Lieutenant Frazier in command. Through some unknown circumstance this officer was also called away, when the command devolved on Ensign Ward. On the 16th of April, a large French force appeared before the fort, under the command of M. de Contrecoeur, and immediately sent a written summons for its surrender. As Ensign Ward had but forty-one available men, and no cannon, acquiescence to the demand was almost imperative. On the 17th the fort was given up, but not until highly honorable terms were obtained from the enemy. At this time, a Virginia regiment under Col. Fry, with George Washington as lieutenant colonel, was at Wills creek, Maryland, on its way to the forks. When the news of the French advance was heard, Washington dispatched a messenger to the governor of Pennsylvania with a dispatch, an extract of which is as follows:

"HONORABLE SIR: It is with the greatest concern I acquaint you that Mr. Ward, ensign in Captain Trent's company, was compelled to surrender his small fort in the forks of Monongahela, to the French, on the 17th instant, who fell down from Winingo with a fleet of three hundred and sixty batoes and canoes, with upwards of one thousand men and eighteen pieces of artillery, which they planted against the fort, drew up their men, and sent the enclosed summons to Mr. Ward, who having but an inconsiderable number of men, and no cannon, to make a proper defence, was obliged to surrender. They suffered him to draw off his men, arms, and working tools, and gave leave that he might retreat to the inhabitants."

After the surrender, the French enlarged and completed the fort, and named it Fort Du Quesne, in honor of the governor of Canada. During the remainder of the year, Captain Trent, with his command, continued at the Virginia camp. In December, he was sent to George Croghan's with messages for a number of French Indians who had arrived there.

In 1755, Captain Trent entered the service of Pennsylvania, having been appointed by Governor R. H. Morris,* a member of the Proprietary and Governor's Council. The following refers to Braddock's defeat. Captain Trent was mistaken in supposing the General had escaped the carnage of that dreadful day:

"Mouth of Conicocheegue,
"Wednesday, *July* 16, 1755.

"*May it please your Honor:*

"Being informed that you were on your journey for the army, but stopped at Shippensburg on account of the news brought by the waggoners, who ran off at the beginning of the engagement, makes me take this opportunity of acquainting your Honor that, by a young man just come here from the camp, we are informed that our army is beat and the artillery taken; but that the General, with the rest of the army, are making a good retreat. As the person who brings this account

---

*Robert Hunter Morris was a son of Governor Lewis Morris, of New Jersey. He was for twenty-six years one of the executive council of that colony, and acquired distinction as a lawyer. From October, 1754, until August, 1756, he was lieutenant governor of Pennsylvania. While acting in that capacity, he also held the place of chief justice of New Jersey, which he resigned in 1757. Died February 20, 1764.

is a sober young man, and came from Fort Cumberland
since an express arrived from the army. I think his account the best to be depended upon; and I imagine
there will be no great danger going to the fort, whers I
intend to set out for this afternoon.

> " I am your Honor's most ob't serv't,
>> "WILLIAM TRENT.
" To the Honorable ROBT. H. MORRIS, Esq."

When the remnant of Braddock's army reached the
mouth of Wills creek, or Fort Cumberland, Captain
Trent rendered efficient service in caring for the wounded
and assisting in the reorganization of the several corps,
a task assigned him by Colonel Washington. Soon
after his return to Pennsylvania, we find him addressing the governor as follows:

> " MOUTH OF CONICOCHEEGUE,
>> "SATURDAY, *October* 4, 1755.

" *Sir:* Last night came to the mill at Wolgomoths,
an express going to the governor of Maryland, with an
account of the inhabitants being out on Paterson's
creek, and about the fort. The express says there is
forty killed and taken, and that one whole family was
burnt to death in a house. The Indians destroy all before them—firing houses, barns, stockyards, and everything that will burn. Jenny McClane, the girl that
lived with Frazier, was taken just by the fort; the man
that was with her had his horse shot through, but it

carried him off; the mischief was all done partly at one time, Wednesday, between eight and ten o'clock in the forenoon. All the inhabitants back are flying. I expect we shall soon be the frontier. My compliments to Mrs. Burd, and

> " I am, Sir, your most humble servant,
>> " WILLIAM TRENT.

" SUNDAY MORNING.—Since I wrote the above, I see another express has come down to get the militia to raise. He says two-and-forty they buried on Paterson's creek, within a few miles of the mouth; they durst not venture higher up, but as there is no word from any of them, without doubt they are all killed; and since they have killed more, and keep on killing, the woods is alive with them. How long will those in power, by their quarrels, suffer us to be massacred? It's time for everybody to provide for the safety of their families.

> " I am, Sir, yours,
>> " W. T."

Early in the year 1757, we find Trent again in the employ of Virginia. In June, he was at Winchester raising men for the army. A month later, at the request of Colonel George Croghan, he acted as his secretary at the council with the Indians, at Easton, Pennsylvania. In 1758, he accompanied Forbes' expedition against Fort Du Quesne, and by his thorough knowledge of the country through which the army passed rendered

important services.   During the year 1759, Captain
Trent entered the service of Sir William Johnson, the
King's Indian agent in America.   In July, he acted as
assistant to George Croghan, deputy agent, at a treaty
made at Fort Pitt with Ohio Indians.   He was also
present, in the same capacity, at General Stanwix's conference with the Western nations in October.

From this time until the year 1763, we have little
regarding his history.

The conspiracy of Pontiac was a terrible misfortune
to Captain Trent.   He had a large trading house near
Fort Pitt, which was plundered and destroyed.   He
likewise lost a large amount of goods, which had been
carried by his agents into the Indian country.   This
was his second misfortune of the kind since the beginning of the war in 1755, and he was totally ruined by it.
Some years later, October, 1768, when a council of the
English, and the Six Nations, Shawanees, and Delawares
was held at Fort Stanwix, New York, Captain Trent
attended.   It was through these Indians that he had
been reduced to poverty, and a favorable opportunity
was presented of obtaining reparation.   Trent not only
represented his own interests, but those of twenty-two
other traders, who had been like sufferers.   Through
the influence of Sir William Johnson and others, the
Indians were induced (November 3, 1768) to make a
deed of land to Trent, in payment of his own claims
and those he represented.   This was satisfactory.   The

tract thus conveyed was situated between the Kanawha and Monongahela rivers. Trent and most of those interested with him soon afterward settled there. We do not again hear of Captain Trent until the breaking out of hostilities with Great Britain. From the beginning of the troubles he warmly advocated the American cause. Congress gave him a major's commission to raise a force in Western Pennsylvania. Of his success we have no information, but we find him present, bearing the title of major, at the treaty of Fort Pitt, July 6, 1776. It is probable he did not long survive that event, as we find no mention of his name afterward.

Major Trent was not a learned man, but was esteemed a careful, prudent, and watchful guardian of the interests of his employers. Most of his life was spent in the public service. His misfortunes were frequent and of the most crushing nature. At one time the Assembly of Pennsylvania passed a bill for his relief, which was approved by the governor; but when it came before the King and Council, was declared null and void.

GOVERNOR ROBERT DINWIDDIE

Board of Trade, October 6, 1752.

"WILLIAMSBURG,* VIRGINIA, *October* 6, 1752.

" *My Lords :* By this ship I transmit to your Lordships a duplicate of the laws passed here last Assembly, for His Majesty's approbation; as also, the other papers, agreeable to my instructions, which I wish safe to your hands. And in that box I also send the copy of report of the commissioners† that delivered His Majesty's present to the several nations of Indians, at Logstown,‡ on the Ohio, to which I beg to be referred. I beg leave to observe that the Twightwees, a large nation

---

* In James City county, Virginia, 58 miles from Richmond. It is the oldest incorporated town in Virginia, and was the seat of government from 1698 until 1779.

† These were Colonel Joshua Fry, Colonel Lunsford Lomax, and Colonel James Patten.

‡ Logstown was on the north bank of the Ohio, fourteen miles northwest of Pittsburg. It had long been a trading point of importance. Many important councils with the Ohio Indians were held there.

of Indians to the westward of the river Ohio, have taken up the hatchet (as they term it) against the French and the Indians in amity with them; that is, that they have declared war against the French and their allies, and that they solicited the friendship of the English and the nations of Indians on the Ohio; as this application was made before His Majesty's present was divided, the commissioners (I think) prudently laid aside part of the present for the Twightwees, which was much approved of by the other nations of Indians then at Logstown, and they sent two gentlemen with that present, to be delivered to the chiefs in the name of His Majesty, the King of Great Britain. This nation of Indians lie a great way west of the Ohio, upon the Lake Erie; they and their allies can bring into the field, as I am informed, at least 10,000* men, and are much more numerous than the Six Nations and all their allies. It's in the power of the Twightwees to stop, and prevent the French having any intercourse between the Mississippi and Canada.† They have towns on the northwest and southwest of the Lake Erie, where the

---

*A mistake—the Miamis could then muster about one thousand warriors.

† The French had a road from Detroit to Fort Miami, at the junction of the Maumee and St. Joseph; thence to the Lower Shawanees town on the Ohio, at the mouth of the Scioto. There was also a trail from Fort Miami to Fort Ouiatenon on the Wabash. The country through which these roads passed was within the boundaries of the Miami territory.

French are obliged to pass in their going from Canada to the Southward. The gentlemen* that carried the present are not yet returned; when they do, I shall write you more fully on this subject. At present I will do all in my power to make a confirmed peace with that nation of Indians, but that must be done by presents; and as they are now at war with the French they will be the easier prevailed on to come into amity with the British nation. I am endeavoring to procure a true account of all the nations of Indians to the west of our settlements, and their number, which, when I have obtained, shall transmit the same to you. I assure you, ever since my arrival I have been closely employed in settling the affairs of this Dominion in proper order. The first step was that of the commission of the peace; the number of justices on my arrival amounted to very near one thousand, which I have reduced, by the advice of the council, to 525, which is a sufficient number for that duty; the residue will be of service to the colony in other stations. Many of our counties had no officers for the militia; I therefore thought it better to give out new commissions to each county, so as to have our militia in good order, which I hope in a short time to perfect, for we are a very open, extensive country, without any fortifications of any consequence. For the above reasons I hope your Lordships will excuse my not giving you the state of this Dominion, agreeable

* Captain William Trent and Andrew Montour.

to my instructions, but shall, as soon as I possibly can, comply with that order, and every other duty of my appointment.

*   *   *   *   *   *

" I am, with great deference and submission,

" Right Honorable, your Lordships'

" Most obed't and very h'ble serv't,

" ROBERT DINWIDDIE."*

---

* Governor of Virginia, 1752–57; born Scotland about 1690; died at Clifton, England, August 1, 1770. A member of the council as early as 1742, he detected and exposed to the government, while employed as clerk to a collector of customs in the West Indies, an enormous fraud practiced by his principal, for which he was rewarded by receiving the post of surveyor of the customs for the colonies, and afterward the government of Virginia. Worn out with vexation and age, he left the colony in January, 1758, and was charged with converting to his own use £20,000 transmitted through his hands as a compensation to the Virginians for the money they had expended beyond their proportion in the public service—a charge which rests on the unsupported assertions of those who were inimical to him. Under his administration the attempt was made to expel the French from the Ohio and Fort Du Quesne, in which Washington first distinguished himself as a military officer, and Braddock fell. He proved himself a zealous and active officer, although totally ignorant of military affairs. He discovered the capacity of Washington, whom he appointed adjutant general of one of the military districts of Virginia, and sent as a commissioner to the French commander on the Ohio. In 1754, he suggested to the British board of trade the propriety of taxing the colonies for the purpose of raising funds to carry on the war, and, in 1755, was one of the five colonial governors who memorialized the ministry to the same effect.—*F. S. Drake's Amer. Biog. Dict.*

GOVERNOR ROBERT DINWIDDIE

TO THE

Board of Trade, Dec'r 10, 1752.

"WILLIAMSBURG, VIRGINIA, *December* 10, 1752.

" *My Lords:*

* * * * * * *

" Since my last letter to your Lordships, Mr. William Trent, who was sent from the Ohio (by the commissioners from this) to the Twightwees, with part of His Majesty's present for that nation, returned some time since, and enclosed I send your Lordships a copy of his journal there and back to this government, by which you 'll please observe the risk he run, and the miserable condition he found these poor people in; their town taken, and many of their people killed by the French and Indians in amity with them, and many of the English traders ruined, being robbed of their goods, some killed and others carried away prisoners ; and all this, as I am informed, is under the conduct of the French from Canada, or New Orleans, on the Mississippi, the Indians having declared to our traders that the French promised to give them one hundred crowns for every white scalp* they bring them; there are no other white people trading there but the English subjects and the French, so it is obvious they would encourage the Indians to murder our traders in cool blood. (Scalping is cutting the skin round the head, and by the hair drawing it off quite to the eyes.) The French traders from Canada have met our traders in the woods and robbed them of all their skins and goods;† they have applied to me for protection, and power to make reprisals, which I by no means would grant, as we are at peace with the French, but I pray your Lordships' directions how to behave on such applications for the

---

* The governor of Canada authorized the commandant at Detroit to offer a large price for the scalps of English traders. A high premium was promised for those of George Croghan and James Lowry, two very influential Pennsylvania traders.

† This was but the natural consequence. It is well known that at this time the governors of New York, Pennsylvania, and Virginia had paid spies among the Ohio Indians, exciting them to war against the French. The territory occupied by these Indians belonged to the French; their right to it had been recognized since the treaty of Utrecht. It had long been settled with both English and French that "none can trade with Indians except those who are on their own territories." The trading of the English with the Miamis was under licenses issued by the governors of Pennsylvania and Virginia. It was a contraband trade—a usurpation of power, of which the French had good reason to complain.

future, as I think the British subjects are under great oppression and severities from the French traders in their villainous robberies.*   And till the line is run between Pennsylvania and this, His Majesty's Dominion, so as to ascertain our limits, I can not appoint magistrates

---

*While the governor of Virginia was bewailing the atrocities committed by the French, *his* traders were engaged in like business. The Miamis had murdered several *Coureur des Bois* in cold blood, killed eight French soldiers, and tomahawked four slaves belonging to the French settlements in Illinois—all this in the winter of 1751–52! Scalps were frequently sent to the governors of Pennsylvania and Virginia, and rewards openly paid. It was unsafe at this time (1752) for a Frenchman to put his foot on *his own territory.*

By way of comparison, we note Governor Dinwiddie's opinion of *his own* traders :

" Our Indian traders, in general, appear to me to be a set of abandoned wretches."—*Extract from a letter to Governor Hamilton, of Pa., May 21, 1753.*

" I concur with you in opinion that the Indian traders are a very licentious people, and may have been guilty of many bad practices." *Extract, Governor Hamilton to Dinwiddie, May, 1753.*

" Whilst the traders are men of dissolute lives, without prudence or abilities, and whilst the Indians are perpetually kept under the influence of strong liquor, who of either sort can be trusted ? "—*Extract, Hamilton to Dinwiddie, August, 1753.*

" The Indian traders used to buy the transported Irish and other convicts, as servants, to be employed in carrying up their goods among the Indians. Many of these ran away from their masters and joined the Indians. The ill-behavior of these people has always hurt the character of the English among the Indians."—*Hist. West. Pa., Apendix, p.* 90.

to keep the traders in good order, as the Pennsylvanians dispute the right of this government to the river Ohio. Since the arrival of Mr. Trent, as above, the Twightwees have sent one Thomas Burney, express, who brought me a belt of wampum, a scalp of one of the Indians that are at war with them and in the interest of the French, with a calmute pipe (being an emblem of peace with those they send it to), and two letters, copy thereof I here enclose to your Lordships; they are of an odd style, but are copied literally as I received them. I dispatched Burney back to them with a belt of wampum. As the season of the year will not admit of sending them any supplies, have assured them, in the spring I would send them and the Six Nations, their friends and allies, twenty barrels gunpowder, one hundred small arms, and some clothing, etc. These nations are very powerful, and of great consequence to all our settlements on the continent. The Twightwees, and other nations contiguous to them and in friendship with them, I am told, can bring into the field ten thousand fighting men, and as they are now joined in strict friendship with the Six Nations of Indians, I think it will be of great service to confirm them to our interest, as they will be a great protection to our back settlements to the westward, and they are able, from their situation, to hinder an intercourse of trade between the French settlements of Canada with that of the Mississippi behind our colonies; and our Indian traders as-

sure me there never was a time as propitious for the
British colonies as now, to secure these people in our
interest, and to encourage the settling the interior parts
of this Dominion; but this can not be done without
considerable presents to them. Therefore, I would
humbly propose that one thousand pounds from the
quit rents should be invested in goods, agreeable to the
enclosed sketch of goods suitable for them, copy thereof
have sent to Mr. John Hanbury;* if it should prove
agreeable from that fund to grant the above sum, he
being a proper person to purchase and ship the goods,
and this colony will be at the charge of forwarding the
goods to them, which will be a very great expense.
The last present cost this Dominion twelve hundred
pounds this money to deliver it; and indeed, if His
Majesty should be graciously pleased to give these poor
people the above present out of the quit rents, it will
be, in a manner, only lending them the money for their
protection. I doubt not in seven years the quit rents
will increase above one thousand pounds per annum,
as many people will take up land when they are assured
of the friendship of the Indians to the westward of our
settlements, and I know no method of getting their
friendship but by presents, and the thousand pounds
proposed will be but a trifle when divided among the
many different nations. If your Lordships should

* One of the proprietors of the Ohio Company.

agree with me on this head, I hope for your interest
and application in obtaining it, and I am of opinion it
should be done immediately, otherways it will be of no
great consequence or so much wanted as at this period
of time.   I have this affair so much at heart, for the
benefit of Great Britain and the Plantations, and the
great advantages I foresee in cultivating a firm alliance
and friendship with these nations, that if the present be
sent out as proposed, I will go and deliver it to them
in person, as I am told such a thing will be of essential
service and most agreeable to them.   By being present,
I would fain hope and expect to confirm them strongly
to the British interest.*   I must observe to your Lordships that the French have already built, and actually
continue to build, forts from Canada quite to the Mississippi, and that not far from our back settlements.
This string of forts, not far distant from each other,
will, in time, much annoy our back country.   The
Twightwees have declared their resolution to destroy
all those on Lake Erie, which if they do, and we settle
so far back, I doubt not, from our numbers, to make
good our just right to these lands.   There came here a

---

* Governor Dinwiddie, in September, 1752, assured the Ohio Indians
that in the following spring he would proceed to Cheningue (now
Warren, Pa.), with a cavalcade of 800 horses, hold a grand council, and
distribute presents of value.   As the French soon occupied the point
where the governor intended holding his conference, nothing further
was heard of it.

deserter from the French. I prevailed with him to give me an account of their forts, men, etc., which I have enclosed you, but I can not think the French have so many forts, and such a number of forces, particularly regular forces, as this person asserts, tho' the man offered to take his oath to the truth of it, but from this information, I think it's full time we should build some forts of defence. The Indians are fond and solicitous that we should build some forts on the Ohio, etc., and I am of opinion it would be a very proper step. In that case we shall want some small cannon, carriages, and powder, etc., proportionable; to make a beginning, twenty or thirty three pounders would do. If this meets with your Lordships' approbation, an order to the Ordnance would soon furnish them, which, I doubt not, you may obtain, not being of any great value; and the Indians on the Ohio have opened a road from a river that runs into the Ohio to the head of Potomac river, in this Dominion, with a land-carriage only of eighty miles, which will be of great use to our settlers and traders, as also for the conveying of our cannon to proper places on the above river.

" Some time since the emperor of the Cherokees, his empress and only son, two of his generals, and attendants, came to this city. They said they had come through briars, thickets, and great waters to see me. I bid them welcome, and assured them of civil entertainment. His errand, I found, was to cultivate a friendship, and encourage a trade from this government to his nation. I told him it was too great a distance from this, as he had come seven hundred miles, and recommended him to continue their trade with South Carolina, which is within one hundred miles of his nation, but he gave me to understand there was some uneasiness and disputes between him and the governor of South Carolina. I advised him to make up these differences and live in friendship with that colony for the future, and I would use my interest with the governor to establish the same. I told him I had not power over our traders to direct them in their commerce, but would acquaint them of the friendship, protection, and encouragement he was pleased to promise them. I ordered for him, empress, son, generals, and attendants some fine cloths and a handsome present. They went away highly pleased, and fully determined to keep up strict friendship and fidelity with the British nation in general and this government in particular.

" My Lords, I fear the length of this letter may be troublesome to you, but the matters contained therein appear to me so essential to the British nation and His Majesty's colonies on this continent, that I could not properly abbreviate it, and if it appear in the same light to your Lordships I hope I shall be excused; at same time beg leave to assure you while I have the honor to preside here my chief aim shall be to promote the interest, trade of Great Britain, and to encourage the settling our back country. With great gratitude and truth I acknowledge the honor I have had of your countenance and patronage, and remain most sincerely,

"Right Honorable, your Lordships'

"Much obliged and most obd't hu'ble serv't,

"ROBT. DINWIDDIE.

"P. S. I have just now received your Lordships' letter of the 3d June, in regard to the revisals of my instructions. As it will require some time to be exact on that head, I shall in a short time write your Lordships fully thereon."

JOURNAL

OF

Captain William Trent, A. D. 1752.

CAPTAIN TRENT TO GOVERNOR DINWIDDIE.

"*To the Honorable Robert Dinwiddie, Esq., His Majesty's Lieut. Governor and Commander-in-Chief of the Colony of Virginia:*

"MAY IT PLEASE YOUR HONOR: In pursuance to instructions which I received from the Honorable Colonel Joshua Fry,* Colonel Lunsford Lomax,† and

---

* Born at Somersetshire, England; died at the mouth of Wills creek, Maryland, May 31, 1754. Educated at Oxford; he was sometime a professor of mathematics in William and Mary College. Was subsequently a member of the House of Burgesses and a commissioner for running the boundary line between Virginia and North Carolina. Well acquainted with the frontier, he made, with Peter Jefferson, a map of Virginia, and was, in 1752, a commissioner to make a treaty with the Indians at Logstown. His integrity, experience, and knowledge of the Indian character qualified him for the command of the expedition against the French, with which he was intrusted in 1754. He died while conducting it to the Ohio.—*F. S. Drake's American Biog. Dict.*

† Colonel Lunsford Lomax was long in the employ of Virginia, and

Colonel James Patten,* your Honor's commissioners, appointed to deliver His Majesty's present to the Indians at Logstown, to proceed with a present to the Twightwees. An account of that whole affair I beg leave to lay before you, which will appear in the following sheets.

> " I am your Honor's
>> " Most dutiful and obedient servant,
>>> "WILLIAM TRENT."

A JOURNAL OF CAPTAIN WILLIAM TRENT TO THE TWIGHTWEE [MIAMI] INDIANS, 1752.

June the 21st, 1752. We left the Logstown.

25th. We met a white man who had been thirteen days from the Pick town;† he informed us that the French Indians had been there, and that twenty-five families of the Picks or Twightwees had gone back with them to the French.

---

esteemed an active, useful, and energetic officer. He commanded a regiment of Virginia volunteers in the French and English war, 1755 –1763.

* James Patten resided in Augusta county, Virginia. He was a man of prominence among the frontier settlers, and frequently held positions of trust and profit. As early as 1742, he was employed by Virginia in negotiating with the Indians.

† Pickawillany, on Evans' map, 1755, located on west bank of Loramies creek, at its mouth. By map, the distance from Logstown to Pickawillany was 326 miles ; from Wills creek, 456 miles.

27th. We met a Mingoe* man called Powell, who had been then just twenty days from Fort D' Troit,† and ten days before he left the fort three hundred French and Indians had set off, either to persuade the Twightwees back to the French, else to cut them off.

29th. We got to Muskingum,‡ 150 miles from the Logstown, where we met some white men from Hock-hocken,§ who told us the town was taken and all the white men killed, the young Shawanees king having made his escape and brought the news.

July the 2d. We reached Hockhocken where we met with William Ives, who passed by the Twightwee town in the night. He informed us that the white men's houses were all on fire, and that he heard no noise in the fort, only one gun fired, and two or three hollows.

---

* The Mingoes were a branch of the Senecas. They came from Western Pennsylvania and located in Northeast and Eastern Ohio. Their principal town was called Mingo Bottom, on the site of Steubenville, Ohio. They were called the "Iroquois of Ohio."

† Detroit. Sieur De l'Hut erected a fort there in 1685, which was rebuilt in 1701 by M. de Cadillac and called Fort Ponchartrain.

‡ A Mingo town on the north bank of the Tuscarawas, five miles east of the mouth of White Woman's creek, in what is now Coshocton county. In 1751 it contained about one hundred families. Boquet was there in 1764, and Colonel Brodhead led an expedition against it in 1780. The distance from Logstown to Muskingum by the Indian trail was 122 miles.

§ The name Hock-hock-ing signifies *a bottle*. The town was a small place, containing a few Delaware families. The French at one time had a trading post there, called "Margaret's Fort."

3d.   We got to the Meguck,* where we heard much the same news, which made us conclude to go to the lower Shawanees town† with the goods, that we might know the certainty.

6th.   We arrived at the lower Shawanees town, where the Indians received us very kindly, with the firing of guns, and whooping and hollowing, according to their custom, and conducted us to the long house (the council house), where, after they had given us victuals, they inquired the news ; we told them the next day we would let them know everything.   Then Thomas Burney and Andrew McBryer,‡ the only two men that escaped, when the town was attacked, came to us and told us that 240 French and Indians, on the 21st of June, about nine o'clock in the morning, surprised the Indians in the cornfields,§ and that they came so suddenly

---

* A Delaware town of ten families, fifteen miles southwest of Hock-hocken.

† There were two towns of this name, both on the Scioto.   One was at the mouth of the river ; the other somewhere in the neighborhood of Columbus.   Trails from both led to Pickawillany.   In 1751 the town at the mouth of the Scioto contained 300 warriors, and 100 houses, besides a state house or council room 90 feet long.   It was to this town that Captain Trent proceeded after leaving Meguck.

‡ Traders.

§ The Miamis cultivated extensive fields of maize.   Their houses were always well supplied with this valuable article of food.

on them that the white men, who were in their houses, had the utmost difficulty to reach the fort. Three not being able to get to the fort shut themselves up in one of the houses. At this time there were but twenty men and boys in the fort, including the white men. The French and Indians having taken possession of the white men's houses, some of which were within ten yards of the fort, they kept a smart fire on the fort till the afternoon, and had taken the three white men who had shut themselves up in one of the houses. Though they had plenty of arms and ammunition in the house, they could not be prevailed upon by the white men and Indians in the fort to fire a gun, though they encouraged them as much as possible, but as soon as they were taken told how many white men were in the fort. The French and Indians in the afternoon let the Twightwees know that if they would deliver up the white men that were in the fort, they would break up the siege and go home. After a consultation it was agreed by the Indians and whites that as there were so few men, and no water in the fort, it was better to deliver up the white men, with beaver and wampum, to the Indians not to hurt them, than for the fort to be taken, and all to be at their mercy. The white men were delivered up accordingly, except Burney and Andrew, whom the Indians hid. One of the white men that was wounded in the belly, as soon as they got him they stabbed and scalped, and took out his heart

and eat it. Upon receiving the white men they delivered up all the Indian women they had prisoners, and
set off with the plunder they got out of the white men's
houses, amounting to about three thousand pounds.
They killed one Englishman and took six prisoners,
one Mingoe and one Shawanees killed, and three
Twightwees; one of them, the old Pianguisha* king,
called by the English Old Britain,† who, for his attachment to the English, they boiled, and eat him all up.‡

---

* A tribe of the Miamis who dwelt upon the Wabash.   The name
has been variously spelled—Peanguichas, Peanguishas, Pianguishaws,
Piankashaws, Piankeshaws, Piankeshas, etc.

† He was the principal man, or commander-in-chief of the Miamis.
His terrible fate was in revenge for the conduct of the Piankeshaws
during the winter of 1751–2, when they killed and scalped eight
French soldiers near Fort Miami, and took four negro slaves prisoners
in the Illinois country.   The bitter enmity of the French was doubtless increased from the fact that the governor of Virginia had recently
offered a high price for " Canadian scalps."

‡ When the French first visited the Iroquois, one of the customs of
that confederacy was to "roast and eat" prisoners taken in battle.   This
barbarous treatment was common in the Northern tribes, and continued until a comparatively late day, *vide* the following extracts from a
letter dated at Detroit, published in the Newport (R. I.) *Mercury*,
July 9, 1763:

" Was it not very agreeable every day to know of the cutting, and
carving, and boiling, and eating of our companions?   They boiled and
eat Sir Robert Davers, and we are informed by Mr. Pauley, who escaped
the other day, that he had seen an Indian with the skin of Captain
Robertson's arm for a tobacco pouch ! '

7th. Scaruneate, with some more of the Six Nations,* came to us in the morning and asked us if we would go with them, in order to bring the remaining Twightwees this way; we told them that we would; then we went to the long house and showed them our belts, and speeches with each belt. Then the Shawanees† that had been at the Twightwees produced the wampum they brought, on a large black belt, with a scalp tied to the end of it,‡ with this speech:

"BROTHERS: We have struck the French, and we expect that all nations in alliance with us will do the same."

The next was a string of black wampum from the captains and warriors of the Twightwees to the captains and warriors of all nations in alliance with them,

---

* This powerful confederacy was formed in 1539, by a union of the Mohawks, Onondagas, Oneidas, Senecas, and Cayugas. In 1712 they were reinforced by the Tuscaroras, and from that time were known as the Six Nations.

† The Shawanees originally belonged south of the Ohio. Having suffered severely from the Cherokees and Chickasaws, they were invited by the Miamis to their country along the Scioto, but were dispersed by the Iroquois in 1672. They then separated, a portion moving to Carolina and others to Pennsylvania. A few remained in Ohio. About the year 1728, they returned to the Scioto. During the French and English war, 1755–1763, they were active allies of the French. In the Revolutionary war they sided with the British, and were bitterly hostile in the Indian wars which followed.

‡ This signifies the nation was at war and had suffered loss.

letting them know that they put their women and children under their care; that inasmuch as they expect that they would all assist them, and that they had not forgot the league betwixt them.

The next was a large white belt* that the Six Nations had sent them upon their first being friends, which was to let them know the situation they were in was bad, and that they should move from the fort with their own people, or the Six Nations, whoever should come first, that they might be in a place of safety; but back with the French they never would go. They also let them know that in the time of the battle the French and Indians called to them, and told them they were dead, whether they killed them or no, for the English and Six Nations would put them all to death; upon which they made them this answer: "You are liars! You have killed of us all, and we'll be revenged."†

July 12th. We left the lower Shawanees town with twenty-two men and boys, whites and Indians, instead of above a hundred, which we expected, occasioned by a quantity of liquor‡ coming to town. The chief we had belonged to the Six Nations.

---

* An emblem of peace and friendship.

† The Indians were good swearers. That branch of the English tongue they learned to perfection from the traders.

‡ All Indians, male and female, are exceedingly fond of rum, and will get drunk whenever they can secure it.

19th. We lay about twenty miles this side the Pick town. Before we took up we heard three guns. We sent some young men out to discover who they were, but they returned without finding anybody. About midnight some of our people that were awake heard a hollow and two whistles; they waked us, and we lay awake the rest of the night, with our guns in our hands.

20th. We sent two men off in the morning to view the town; they met us about five miles on this side of the town and told us that it was deserted, and that there were two French flags flying. We went to the town, unloaded our horses and turned them into the corn-fields, and hoisted the English colors; we sent out peo-ple to track which way they were gone; they found where two men, the day before, had been sitting in the cornfields, which we suppose to be some of the enemy watching the fort. They found the people's tracks down the creek, one part of which had taken through the woods, for the lower Shawanees town, and the rest had gone towards their own people. We got water in the fort, and secured two of the fort gates; the other we left open for our people to go in and out at. A little after dark we heard three guns fired along the French road, upon which we sent four young men out to scout about the edge of the woods, to see what they could discover, and the rest of us kept awake all night, at the fort gate, with our guns in our hands.

21st.   In the morning we tied up part of the skins that were left in the fort, and lent the man whom the skins belonged to our riding horses to bring them off. We sent some people out along the French road,* but they returned without discovering any of the enemy. They found a blue jacket and a shirt stabbed in six or seven places, all bloody, which we suppose belonged to some of the Indians that were killed.   About noon we set off upon the people's track down the creek.   We went about seven miles, and then took up in order to kill meat, having no provisions but what we killed.

29th.   We reached the Shawanees town after a very tiresome and tedious journey, having then carried the goods between six and seven hundred miles, the weather the hottest that ever was known in these parts, many of the Indian dogs dropping dead as they were hunting; the runs and creeks were so dry, that we were almost perished for want of water, having traveled one day two and twenty miles without a drop.   After we had refreshed ourselves we went to see the Twightwees, and found that the young Pianguisha king, Musheguanock-que, or the Turtle,† two more men, Old Britain's wife

---

* Trail leading to Fort Miami, at the junction of the Maumee and St. Joseph rivers, near where Fort Wayne (Ind.) now stands.

† A Miami chief of this name led the Indians at Hardin's and Wyllys' defeats in Harmar's campaign, 1790, and also at St. Clair's defeat the following year.

and son,* with about a dozen women and their children, were come this way.

August 4th. When the six Cherokees† were coming into town, the Shawanees sent for us to the place they had made to receive them. After we had been there some time they hoisted a suit of French colors, which the French had given to Nucheconner.‡ I got up and told them that I looked upon the hoisting them colors as an affront to his Majesty, the King of Great Britain, and as I was doing the King's business, I could hear no councils under them, upon which Mr. Montour and myself got up and went away. As soon as an Indian, called the Blue Shadow,§ understood it, he struck them, and throwed them away as far as he could throw them.

"Brothers, the Twightwees: We present you with this string of wampum to wash away the blood, and to take

---

* Called Ellonagoa Pyangeacha. At the council at Carlisle, October 3, 1753, the wife of "Old Britain" thus referred to her son: "Remember, brethren, that my husband took a fast hold of the chain of friendship subsisting between your nations. Therefore, I now deliver up his child into your care and protection, and desire you would take care of him, and remember the alliance his father was in with you, and not forget his friendship, but continue kind to his child."

† The Cherokees resided south of the Ohio, to the west of the Carolinas, and, in 1752, numbered about 2,500 warriors.

‡ King of the Shawanees.

§ A Cherokee chief.

away grief from your hearts." [We gave a string of
black and white wampum.]*

The Six Nations then spoke to the Twightwees:
"Brothers, the Twightwees: We present you with this

---

* The use of wampum as a subject of exchange among the early inhabitants of the northern portion of this continent extends back to a
very early period, the antiquity of which can not be determined. It
was probably the first idea of standard values, to the minds of the Indians, in that part of this country now occupied by the Eastern and
Middle States. The primitive wampum consisted of strings, made of
small fresh-water shells. But when the Dutch became fairly settled in
"Manhadoes," New York—when they got the idea of wampum fairly
settled in their minds—they immediately set to work improving upon
its manufacture by making it more beautiful. The beads were of a
purple and white color, about a quarter of an inch in length and an
eighth of an inch in diameter, and holes bored in them lengthwise, so
as to be conveniently strung. The white beads were made from sea-
conch, and the purple from muscle-shell, though not entirely confined
to these shells. Wampum, in the history of that portion of the Indians before mentioned, became an instrument of love, trade, religious
ceremonies, diplomacy, and war ; nothing of importance was done or
said without wampum. They were woven into belts, used singly and in
strings, and were arranged by the color into figures symbolizing objects, events, and acts. Wampum was supplied to the Western Indians
by traders. The use of wampum as money enabled the Dutch to lay
up immense fortunes. What the Dutch did at "Manhadoes," the English and others did farther east, and their examples were not lost upon
their descendants, for gewgaws have followed the Indians in their retreat before civilization, thus giving shadows of value to the Indian for
his substance—the result of war and the chase.—*W. J. Rattle—Ext.
Letter to Editor.*

string of wampum to wipe away your tears, that you may see clearly what we and your brothers, the English, are going to say to you." [Gave a string of black and white wampum.]

The Six Nations spoke again to the Twightwees: " Brothers, the Twightwees: We present you with this string of wampum to clear your hearts and open your minds, that you may understand rightly what your brothers, the English, are going to say to you." [Gave a string of white wampum.]

" Brothers, the Twightwees: We must now inform you that your brothers, the Delawares, desired us to remember the treaty made betwixt us, the Six Nations, the Shawanees, Wyandotts,* and themselves, with you, and they desire that you would go down and brighten the chain, and renew the friendship already made betwixt us,† and they further desire the English and the Six Nations to put their hands upon your heads and keep the French from hurting you, and to advise you not to listen or hear what the French say to you.

" Brethren, you joined in a covenant chain with us,

---

* Once a powerful nation occupying the territory from Lake Erie to the Ohio, between that river and the Great Miami. Their numbers were reduced by repeated wars with the Iroquois, and by that scourge of the red man, the small-pox.

† Treaty at Lancaster, 1748.

your brethren, the English, and the Six United Nations of Indians and their allies, three or four years ago. The King of Great Britain, your father, has now sent a very large present of goods to the Logstown, to be divided amongst his children.   As you could not come thither, we have taken care to send you part.   We join with the Six United Nations of Indians in advising you to stand fast* in the chain of friendship, which you have already taken hold of, and assure you of the friendship of the government of Virginia, under the direction of the great King, your father, on the other side of the water."   [We gave a belt† of wampum.]

The Twightwees made the following speech, with a beaver blanket, with a green painted spot in the middle:

" Brothers : We perceive that your country is all smooth and clear like this blanket, and that your hearts are good, and the dwellings of your governors are like this green painted spot in the middle of the blanket, which represents the Spring in its bloom."   [Gave the beaver blanket.]

The Six Nations then produced a large belt, which the

---

* That is, go on in the good work; act vigorously, etc.; remain true to the English.

† Among the Indians the size of the belts they give with their speeches, is always in proportion to their ideas of the greater or less importance of the matters treated of.

Twightwees had sent to all the nations in alliance with them, with the following speech :

" Brothers : We are very sorry that our people were so foolish as to deliver the English out of the fort to the French and their Indians, but as our people first consulted the English in the fort, and it was agreed that it was better to deliver them up (which we did, with beaver and wampum, to the Indians, not to hurt them), than all to be killed, and we desire all our friends to speak to our brothers, the English, and to intercede with them not to desert us, but send their traders amongst us, and pity our women and children." [Showed the belt.]

The Six Nations made the following speech to the Twightwees, with a belt of white wampum, in favor of themselves and the English :

" Brothers : We desire you to be strong, and to hold fast the chain of friendship concluded between us, you, and the English, and we desire you not to mind that the French and their Indians may say to our disadvantage, for you have now once more come amongst us, and you now see what some of your own people that loved the French told you, that we should put you to death if you came amongst us, is all lies. You have now an opportunity of seeing that we are still your friends, and of being assured, from our own mouths, that we shall always remain so ; and we would have you mind what your brothers, the Delawares,* shall say to you, for they have been long acquainted with the English and know their hearts." [Gave the belt.]

Then the Twightwees produced a feathered pipe, and made the following speech :

"Brothers : We now acquaint you that the French and their Indians have struck us, yet we kept this pipe whole and unhurt ; that is as much as to say, they still hold fast of the chain of friendship with the English, Six Nations, and their allies." [Gave the pipe to the Six Nations.]

The Six Nations then made the following speech to the Twightwees, with a string of black and white wampum :

"Brothers : We are glad to see that you have kept safe that pipe,† by which we see you have not forgot the treaty between you, us, and the English." [Gave the string.]

Then the Six Nations gave us a twist of tobacco‡ to

---

* An Eastern tribe, who were at the beginning of the eighteenth century located in Eastern Pennsylvania.

"About the year 1724, the Delaware Indians, for the conveniency of game, emigrated (from Delaware river and Susquehanna) to the branches of the Ohio. * * * They were soon met by Canadian traders, and *Joncaire*, the adopted citizen of the Seneca nation, found his way to them from Lake Erie."—*Bancroft's U. S.*

† The Indians smoke in their councils.

‡ The giving of tobacco means that the Indians desire to be allies and live in friendship and good will toward each other.

be given to the Half King,† to desire him to acquaint the Six Nations of what had been done at the Twightwees, and to desire him to come down and see what they would do with them.

Then the Shawanees produced a shell and black string of wampum from the Twightwees, acquainting all nations in alliance with them that they had but one heart with them, and though it was darkness to the westward, yet toward the sun-rising it was bright and clear.† [Gave the shell and string to be given the Six Nations.]

Then the Shawanees produced a string of mostly black wampum from the captains and warriors of the Twightwees, letting the captains and warriors of all nations in alliance with them know that their hands had been tied, but now they were loose, and that they have the hatchet in their hands ready to strike the French and their Indians, and they desire all their friends to

---

* A name given by the English to the celebrated Seneca chief, *Tanacharisson*. He was an active friend of the English. In 1753, he accompanied Washington to Fort Le Boeuf, and kept the governor of Pennsylvania fully advised as to subsequent movements of the French. While at Harris' Ferry (Harrisburg) he was " suddenly seized with a violent sickness," which ended his life in a few hours, October 1, 1754. The loss of this chief was a serious one to the English. Had he lived, he would have been of great service in Braddock's short campaign.

† Means war to the westward with the French, peace in the east with the English.

assist them.   [Gave the string to be given to the Six
Nations.]

Then the Twightwees produced a black and white
string of wampum, letting the Shawanees and Delawares
know that when they went there before, they had cleared
a road, but as it had been stopped by the French and
Indians, they now clear it again.   [Gave the string of
wampum.]

Then the old Pianguisha king's wife got the following speech made to all nations in alliance with them,
with a string of black and white wampum:

"Brothers: The French have killed my husband.   I
am now left a poor, lonely woman, with one son, who
I recommend to the care of the English, Six Nations,
Shawanees, and Delawares, and desire they will take
care of him."   [Gave the Six Nations the string.]

Then the Delawares produced a feathered pipe, and
beaver blanket from the Wawetannes,* with the following speech to the English, Six Nations, and their allies:

" Brothers: We have had this pipe from the beginning of the world, and whenever it got cloudy we sweep
the clouds away, and though it is dark to the westward,
yet we sweep all clouds away towards the sun-rising, and
leave a clear and serene sky; and, brothers, we present
you with this beaver blanket, hoping that your hearts

---

* A tribe of the Miamis, sometimes called Ouiatenons, who resided
on the Wabash.

and minds may be as clear as the green painted spot in the middle." [Gave the pipe and blanket to be given to the Six Nations.]

The Twightwees made the following speech to the English, with a green belt and pipe:

" Brothers: When we first went to see you, we made a road* which reached to your country, which road the

---

* This refers to the trail from Pickawillany to the mouth of Wills creek; the following is a description of its course:

Beginning at mouth of Wills creeк or Fort Cumberland; thence northwesterly over the Alleghany mountains forty-one miles to the forks of the Youghiogheny; thence southwest along the base of Laurel Hill twelve miles to Great Meadows, which is near the Pennsylvania line; thence northwest, over Laurel Hill, to Christopher Gist's house, eight miles; thence in the same course six miles to Stewart's cabin or crossing on the Youghiogheny; crossing the Youghiogheny to the north bank and following a course generally parallel with that stream forty-one miles to the forks of the Ohio, where Pittsburg now stands; crossing the Alleghany at its mouth along or near the Ohio river twenty miles to Logstown; thence westerly down the Ohio river, crossing the Big Beaver at eight miles at Shingoes town, and pursuing the same general direction westward, crossing the waters of the Little Beaver and head waters of Yellow creek into the valley of the Big Sandy to Tuscarawas town, a distance of seventy miles; from Tuscarawas town, six miles above the mouth of the Big Sandy, on the north bank, the trail crossed this stream and followed down the eastern shore of the Tuscarawas river, six miles, to Three Legs town, and thence parallel with the Tuscarawas to Muskingum, an Indian town between the forks of the Muskingum; thence westerly across the Walhonding, a distance of three miles, to White Woman's town; thence pursuing the same course

French and Indians have made bloody; now we make a new road, which reaches all the way to the sun-rising, one end of which we will hold fast, which road shall remain open and clear forever, that we and our brothers may travel backwards and forwards to one another with safety; and if we live till the Spring, our brothers may expect to see us, and we send this pipe that our brothers may smoke out of, and think upon what we say, and they may depend upon seeing us in the Spring, at which time we will give a full answer." [Gave the belt and pipe.]

Speeches made to the Shawanees by the six Cherokees, who came to make peace with the Six Nations and their allies:

" Brethren: We give you this tobacco to smoke, that while you are smoking you may consider us and pity our condition." [Gave some tobacco tied in a piece of leather.]

---

westerly, crossing the Licking above Newark, to Hockhocken or French Margaret's town, on the head waters of the Hockhocking river, a distance of seventy-two miles; continuing westerly across the waters of the Scioto, above the town of the Delawares, which is at the forks across the head waters of the Little Miami and Mad rivers, to the Great Miami, at the mouth of Loramies creek, a distance, according to Evans' map, of one hundred and two miles, where was situated the Twightwee town or English fort of Pickawillany; from thence it continued a course nearly due west to the Wawixtas town on the Wabash, a distance of ninety miles.

" Brethren: We are come to inform you that four-teen hundred of our men will be here in about two months, to live amongst you, for we can live no longer in our own country, for the English are angry and re-fuse to supply us with powder and lead, because they say we kill their traders. [Gave a string of white beads.]

"Brethren: We are sensible there has been a great many traders killed, but we have not done it. You know that it is the French Indians that have killed them, therefore we beg that you, the Six Nations, and Delawares, would intercede with our brothers, the En-glish, for us, that they may take pity upon our women and children, and not desert us, but that they may take us under their protection." [Gave a string of white wampum.]

All the speeches that were delivered to the Six Na-tions by the Shawanees and Delawares that came from the Twightwees, and those from the deputies of the Six Nations, were delivered again to the head men of the Six Nations, at the Logstown, by Mr. Andrew Mon-tour,* in order that they might send some person to the

---

* Andrew Montour was an interpreter, at times in the employ of Pennsylvania and Virginia. He also officiated as a spy among the In-dians on various occasions. His influence was confined to the Senecas, Delawares, and Shawanees. He was a son of the celebrated Canadian half-breed, Catharine Montour. Stone, in his life of Brant, I. 340, thus refers to her history: "She was a native of Canada, a half-breed,

head council at Onondagoa* with them. When we found that Old Britain was killed, we gave the cloths, by advice of the Six Nations, in the following manner: The scarlet cloak to Old Britain's son, a young lad ; the hat and jacket, with the shirt and stockings, to the young Pianguisha king; we clothed Old Britain's wife, and gave the rest of the goods to the young Pianguisha king, the Turtle, and two more men of the nation, for the use of the Twightwees; and I

---

her father having been one of the early French governors—probably Count Frontenac, as he must have been in the government of that country at about the time of her birth. During the wars between the Six Nations and the French and Hurons, Catharine, when about ten years of age, was made a captive, taken into the Seneca country, adopted, and reared as one of their own children. When arrived at a suitable age she was married to one of the distinguished chiefs of her tribe, who signalized himself in the wars of the Six Nations against the Catawbas, then a great nation living southwestward of Virginia. She had several children by this chieftain, who fell in battle about the year 1750, after which she did not marry again. She is said to have been a handsome woman when young, genteel and of polite address, notwithstanding her Indian associations. It was frequently her lot to accompany the Six Nations to Philadelphia and other places in Pennsylvania where treaties were holden ; and, from her character and manners, she was greatly caressed by the American ladies, particularly in Philadelphia, where she was invited by the ladies of the best circles, and entertained at their houses. Her residence was at the head of Seneca Lake." Andrew had a brother Henry, who was an intelligent Indian, and frequently in employ of the governors.

* Onondaga, Onondaga county, New York.

persuaded an Indian trader to carry the goods for them, who promised to do it, and he set off with horses for the lower Shawanees town for that purpose.

N. B. The young Pianguisha king,* and Musheguanockque, or the Turtle, were two of the deputies for the Twightwees when they first entered into an alliance with the English.†

While we were at the lower Shawanees town, there came a messenger from the Six Nations to order the Indians there to keep themselves together, and to acquaint them there was an army from Canada arrived in the lakes.

WILLIAM TRENT.

---

* His Indian name was Assapausa.

† The deputies at the treaty at Lancaster were Ciquenackqua, Assapausa, and Natoecqueha.

THE LORDS OF TRADE

TO

Governor Robt. Dinwiddie, Jan. 17, 1753.

1753, JANUARY 17. LETTER TO ROBERT DINWIDDIE, ESQ., LIEUT. GOVERNOR OF VIRGINIA, IN ANSWER TO ONE FROM HIM OF THE 6TH OCTOBER LAST.

"*To Robert Dinwiddie, Esq., Lieut. Governor of Virginia:*

"SIR: We have received your letter of the 6th of October last, in which you acquaint us that the Twightwees, a large nation of Indians to the westward of the river Ohio, have declared war against the French and the Indians in amity with them, and have solicited the friendship of the English, and that this application having been made before His Majesty's present was divided, the commissioners laid aside a part of the present for the Twightwees.

"As the friendship of so powerful an Indian nation as you represent the Twightwees to be is of very great importance, not only to the colony under your government in particular, but to the British interest in North America in general, we approve the conduct of the commissioners in reserving for them a part of His

Majesty's present, and we make no doubt but you will do everything in your power to secure their friendship and fidelity.

"We commend your assiduity in establishing good order and government in the affairs of the colony, and we doubt not but the good effects of your endeavors will appear in the state of Virginia, which you promise to transmit to us as soon as you possibly can.

  *   *   *   *   *   *

"So we bid you heartily farewell, and are
  "Your very loving friends,
      "DUNK HALIFAX,
       CHAS. TOWNSHEND,
       JAMES OSWALD,
       JOHN PITT.

"P. S. We have not as yet received the box, in which you mention to have sent the report of the commissioners who delivered the presents to the Indian nations, some acts, and other public papers."

THE LORDS OF TRADE

Earl of Holdernesse, March 16, 1753.

1753, MARCH 16TH. LETTER TO THE EARL OF HOLDER-
NESSE, INCLOSING AN EXTRACT OF ONE FROM MR. DIN-
WIDDIE, LIEUT. GOVERNOR OF VIRGINIA, TO THE
BOARD, AND COPIES OF OTHER PAPERS THEREIN MEN-
TIONED.

"*Right Honorable, Earl of Holdernesse, one of His Majesty's Principal Secretaries of State :*

"MY LORD : We have lately received a letter from
Robert Dinwiddie, Esq., Lieut. Governor of His Majesty's Colony, Virginia, dated the 10th December, 1752,
in which he gives us an account, amongst other things,
that the Indians inhabiting the western parts of that
province, who are in friendship and alliance with His
Majesty, have lately been attacked by the French and
Indians in amity with them, who have committed acts
of great cruelty and violence, and robbed and plundered

several of His Majesty's subjects who carry on a trade with the said Indians.   Mr. Dinwiddie likewise transmits to us an account given to him by a deserter, of the number and strength of the forts built by the French to secure a communication between Canada and New Orleans, on the Mississippi.   These matters appear to us to be of great consequence, and we can not but express our fears and apprehensions that unless some measures be speedily taken to put a stop to these proceedings and encroachments of the French, any further attempts of His Majesty's subjects to make settlements in the interior part of America will be effectually prevented; their trade and commerce with the Indians rendered very hazardous and precarious, by an alienation of their affections from the British interest, and in case of any future rupture between the two crowns, His Majesty's provinces will be greatly exposed to their ravages and incursions.   We have, therefore, thought it our duty to transmit to your Lordship an extract of so much of Mr. Dinwiddie's letter as relates to this point, together with copies of several papers referred to in it, and to desire your Lordship will be pleased to lay them before His Majesty; and as it appears to be a matter of a very tender nature, and we are entirely unacquainted with the state of the negotiations at present carried on between the two crowns with respect to the disputes in America, we must submit to His Majesty's wisdom what directions may be proper to be given upon this occasion.

"We are, my Lord, your Lordship's

"Most obed't and most humble serv'ts,

"DUNK HALIFAX,

J. GRENVILLE,

DUPPLIN.

"WHITEHALL, *March* 16, 1753."

FINIS.

INDEX.

Abenaquis, 17.
Albany, N. Y., 11.
America, Management of Colonies in, III.
Arnaud, M. de, 14.
Arowin, Luke, 33.
Assapausa, a Piankeshaw chief, 23; signs treaty at Lancaster, 105.

Beautiful River, a name applied to the Ohio, 26.
Belle-riviere, French name for the Ohio, 26.
Belletre, Monsieur, 44.
Bellomont, Earl, Governor of New York, 9.
Biographical Notices: Charlevoix, 13; Clarke, George Rogers, 55; Clinton, George, 57; Cornbury, Lord, 10; Croghan, George, 28; Dinwiddie, Robert, 72; Frontenac, Count de, 7; Fry, Joshua, 83; Hamilton, James, 27; Hennepin, Louis, 6; Johnson, Sir William, 25; Lomax, Lunsford, 83; Montour, Andrew, 103; Morris, Robert Hunter, 63; Old Britain, 88; Patten, James, 84; Tanacharisson, or Half King, 99; Thomas, George, 57; Trent, William, 57; Weiser, Conrad, 41.
Blue Shadow, a Cherokee chief, 93.
Bois Blanc Island, 17.
Borke, Thomas, 33.
Braddock's defeat, 63, 64, 99.
Bradstreet, Colonel, 36.
British State Paper Office, III.
Burney, Thomas, 46, 47, 48, 49, 76, 86.

Cadillac, M. de, commandant at Detroit, 9, 11.
Callender, Robert, 46, 48, 53.
Campbell, Colonel, 37.
Canada, Governor of, 6, 12, 45.
Caravans, 43.
Carlisle, Pa., council at, 34, 50.
Catawbas, 104.
Cayugas, 89.

Celeron, M. de, leads expedition to Ohio Country, 25, 27; objects of, 26; visits the Miamis, 26; at Pickawillany, 40.
Cequenackqua, a Miami chief, 23, 105.
Chaouenons, 17.
Charlevoix, 13; biographical sketch of, 13.
Cheningue (now Warren, Pa.), 78.
Cherokees, 79, 89, 93, 102; emperor of visits Dinwiddie, 80.
Chicago, 6.
Chicagon, 13.
Chickasaws, 89.
Chippewas, 37, 46, 50.
Chippewas and Ottawas, notice of, 46.
Clarke, George Rogers, destroys Loramies Station, 55; biographical sketch of, 55.
Clinton, George, Governor of New York, 57; biographical sketch of, 57.
Contrecoeur, M. de, 61.
Cornbury, Lord, 10; biographical sketch of, 10.
Courcelles, 7.
Coureurs des Bois, 39, 75.
Crawford, Hugh, 27, 30.
Croghan, George, 28, 32, 33, 35, 37, 41, 44, 45, 5 ., 53, 58, 61, 63, 65, 66, 74; biographical sketch of, 28.
Cumberland, Fort, 64, 101.
Cuyahoga, 28.

Davers, Sir Robert, boiled and eaten, 88.
Delawares, 22, 34, 51, 59, 60, 66, 95, 98, 100, 103.
Delaware Town, 102.
Detroit, 5, 10, 15, 33; commandant at, 11, 16, 45; conspiracy of Nicholas discovered at, 18; plan for capture of, 17; when settled, 85.
Detroit Hurons, precipitate action of, 18.
Dinwiddie, Robert, Governor of Virginia, 59, 60, 72, 75, 107, 109, 110; biographical sketch of, 72.
Dubuisson, Sieur, 17, 20.

The First American Frontier
AN ARNO PRESS/NEW YORK TIMES COLLECTION

Agnew, Daniel.
A History of the Region of Pennsylvania North of the Allegheny River. 1887.

Alden, George H.
New Government West of the Alleghenies Before 1780. 1897.

Barrett, Jay Amos.
Evolution of the Ordinance of 1787. 1891.

Billon, Frederick.
Annals of St. Louis in its Early Days Under the French and Spanish Dominations. 1886.

Billon, Frederick.
Annals of St. Louis in its Territorial Days, 1804-1821. 1888.

Littel, William.
Political Transactions in and Concerning Kentucky. 1926.

Bowles, William Augustus.
Authentic Memoirs of William Augustus Bowles. 1916.

Bradley, A. G.
The Fight with France for North America. 1900.

Brannan, John, ed.
Official Letters of the Military and Naval Officers of the War, 1812-1815. 1823.

Brown, John P.
Old Frontiers. 1938.

Brown, Samuel R.
The Western Gazetteer. 1817.

Cist, Charles.
Cincinnati Miscellany of Antiquities of the West and Pioneer History. (2 volumes in one). 1845-6.

Claiborne, Nathaniel Herbert.
Notes on the War in the South with Biographical Sketches of the Lives of Montgomery, Jackson, Sevier, and Others. 1819.

Clark, Daniel.
Proofs of the Corruption of Gen. James Wilkinson. 1809.

Clark, George Rogers.
Colonel George Rogers Clark's Sketch of His Campaign in the Illinois in 1778-9. 1869.

Collins, Lewis.
Historical Sketches of Kentucky. 1847.

Cruikshank, Ernest, ed,
Documents Relating to Invasion of Canada and the Surrender of Detroit. 1912.

Cruikshank, Ernest, ed,
The Documentary History of the Campaign on the Niagara Frontier, 1812-1814. (4 volumes). 1896-1909.

Cutler, Jervis.
A Topographical Description of the State of Ohio, Indian Territory, and Louisiana. 1812.

Cutler, Julia P.
The Life and Times of Ephraim Cutler. 1890.

Darlington, Mary C.
History of Col. Henry Bouquet and the Western Frontiers of Pennsylvania. 1920.

Darlington, Mary C.
Fort Pitt and Letters From the Frontier. 1892.

De Schweinitz, Edmund.
The Life and Times of David Zeisberger. 1870.

Dillon, John B.
History of Indiana. 1859.

Eaton, John Henry.
Life of Andrew Jackson. 1824.

English, William Hayden.
Conquest of the Country Northwest of the Ohio. (2 volumes in one). 1896.

Flint, Timothy.
Indian Wars of the West. 1833.

Forbes, John.
Writings of General John Forbes Relating to His Service in North America. 1938.

Forman, Samuel S.
Narrative of a Journey Down the Ohio and Mississippi in 1789-90. 1888.

Haywood, John.
Civil and Political History of the State of Tennessee to 1796. 1823.

Heckewelder, John.
History, Manners and Customs of the Indian Nations. 1876.

Heckewelder, John.
Narrative of the Mission of the United Brethren. 1820.

Hildreth, Samuel P.
Pioneer History. 1848.

Houck, Louis.
The Boundaries of the Louisiana Purchase: A Historical Study. 1901.

Houck, Louis.
History of Missouri. (3 volumes in one). 1908.

Houck, Louis.
The Spanish Regime in Missouri. (2 volumes in one). 1909.

Jacob, John J.
A Biographical Sketch of the Life of the Late Capt. Michael Cresap. 1826.

Jones, David.
A Journal of Two Visits Made to Some Nations of Indians on the West Side of the River Ohio, in the Years 1772 and 1773. 1774.

Kenton, Edna.
Simon Kenton. 1930.

Loudon, Archibald.
Selection of Some of the Most Interesting Narratives of Outrages. (2 volumes in one). 1808-1811.

Monette, J. W.
History, Discovery and Settlement of the Mississippi Valley. (2 volumes in one). 1846.

Morse, Jedediah.
American Gazetteer. 1797.

Pickett, Albert James.
History of Alabama. (2 volumes in one). 1851.

Pope, John.
A Tour Through the Southern and Western Territories. 1792.

Putnam, Albigence Waldo.
History of Middle Tennessee. 1859.

Ramsey, James G. M.
Annals of Tennessee. 1853.

Ranck, George W.
Boonesborough. 1901.

Robertson, James Rood, ed.
Petitions of the Early Inhabitants of Kentucky to the Gen. Assembly of Virginia. 1914.

Royce, Charles.
Indian Land Cessions. 1899.

Rupp, I. Daniel.
History of Northampton, Lehigh, Monroe, Carbon and Schuykill Counties. 1845.

Safford, William H.
The Blennerhasset Papers. 1864.

St. Clair, Arthur.
A Narrative of the Manner in which the Campaign Against the Indians, in the Year 1791 was Conducted. 1812.

Sargent, Winthrop, ed.
A History of an Expedition Against Fort DuQuesne in 1755. 1855.

Severance, Frank H.
An Old Frontier of France. (2 volumes in one). 1917.

Sipe, C. Hale.
Fort Ligonier and Its Times. 1932.

Stevens, Henry N.
Lewis Evans: His Map of the Middle British Colonies in America. 1920.

Timberlake, Henry.
The Memoirs of Lieut. Henry Timberlake. 1927.

Tome, Philip.
Pioneer Life: Or Thirty Years a Hunter. 1854.

Trent, William.
Journal of Captain William Trent From Logstown to Pickawillany. 1871.

Walton, Joseph S.
Conrad Weiser and the Indian Policy of Colonial Pennsylvania. 1900.

Withers, Alexander Scott.
Chronicles of Border Warfare. 1895.